EVERY THURSDAY

A warm, loving look at
GRANDPARENTING

BILL & PAT COLEMAN

Requests for permission to quote from this book should be
directed to: Permissions Department, Discovery House Publishers,
P.O. Box 3566, Grand Rapids, MI 49501.

Discovery House Publishers is affiliated with
RBC Ministries, Grand Rapids, Michigan 49501.

Discovery House books are distributed to the trade exclusively
by Barbour Publishing, Inc., Uhrichsville, OH 44683.

Unless otherwise indicated, Scripture is taken from
the Holy Bible, New International Version (NIV), ©1973, 1978,
1984 by International Bible Society. Used by permission.

Interior design by Sherri L. Hoffman

Library of Congress Cataloging-in-Publication Data

Coleman, William L.
Every Thursday : a warm, loving look at grandparenting / by
    William and Patricia Coleman.
    p. cm.
    ISBN: 1-57293-120-5
Grandparents—Religious life. 2. Grandparenting—Religious
    aspects—Christianity. I. Coleman, Patricia. II. Title.
BV4528.5.C65 2004
248.8'45—dc22

                                                    2003024986

Printed in the United States of America
04 05 06 07 08 09 / PP /10 9 8 7 6 5 4 3 2

For
Evan, Ian, Emma, Erin, Nolan

The people whom the sons and daughters find hardest to understand are the fathers and mothers, but young people can get on very well with the grandfathers and grandmothers.

SIMEON STRUNSKY

TABLE OF CONTENTS

Part 8: For My Grandchildren I Will . . .

Introduction

OUR FAVORITE DAY

🌀

This is the day the LORD *has made;*
let us rejoice and be glad in it.
—PSALM 118:24

ine years ago, soon after the birth of our first grand-child, we started a new tradition. On our calendars we marked off Thursdays. We didn't, and still don't, take any office appointments. We get up at 6:30, pack lunches, and make coffee-to-go. We lock up the house and leave the phone to its own devices. Pat drives while Bill reads the newspaper and sips coffee. For the next hour and twenty minutes, we head for our grandchildren's house.

Our Thursdays belong to them. The grandchildren aren't sick or poor. We simply decided to carve out a new trail.

Now, nearly a decade into our adventure, the scenario looks like this: We arrive at nine o'clock, and Bill heads out to McDonald's for breakfast with our nine-year-old grandson. The workers at McDonald's know them by name now. The two draw cartoons and make plans for their morning.

Pat cooks breakfast for our two six-year-old granddaughters and reads to them while they eat. After their morning chores, the three play in the backyard or go biking to the park two blocks away, or they may choose to stay inside and play house or make-believe.

Before noon Bill and our grandson return home, and we sit around the table and eat lunches while Bill tells a made-up story to delight us all.

In the afternoon we split up, a child with each adult—our daughter, Bill, and Pat—taking turns each week, giving us individual time with each child.

On special occasions on summer afternoons, we all head out together for an outing, such as to the swimming pool, indoor playground, park, museum, observatory, or a special event in the city.

We all return to their house in time for the children to have supper with their parents. We two eat out and head for home.

When school starts, we spend four hours with the children, from 4:00 to 8:00 P.M., splitting up, one child with each adult (our daughter, Bill, and Pat).

Thursdays we set our adult responsibilities on the back burner. We forget the bills that are due at the end of the week. Doing stuff together is the sole agenda for the day.

"I like every day when you and Grandpa come," our granddaughter said one day when she was five.

"I like every day when we get to come," Pat quickly replied.

Seven years after our original decision to mark off Thursdays, we were blessed with another happy decision. A beautiful son was born to our daughter and son-in-law in Kansas. He is now two-and-a-half and has a sweet eight-month-old brother.

Again, we pulled out the calendar and marked off every other Monday. Their home in a small rural town is three-and-a-half hours distant from us. We split our time at their home, so we can be one-on-one with each boy.

How can we help our grandchildren? What do their parents need from us? Those may be good questions for most grandparents, but they never worked for us. The reason we began to visit them each week was twofold. First, we wanted to hang out with them so we would know them and they, us.

We wanted to be part of their lives; we wanted them to be part of our lives. Second, we wanted to learn from them what was really important in life. We knew spending time with a child would make us better people.

We're not Big Granddaddy or Grandma bestowing blessings on these small tots. Rather, they are precious children reaching up to infuse our lives with hope, wonder, and purpose.

The joy of interacting with grandchildren is a bonus none of us deserves, but how fortunate we are that God sent these gifts along.

We can only hope that our encounters with our grandchildren will encourage you to get to know, have fun with, and learn from your grandchildren.

This is the day to enjoy grandchildren. Indulge yourself in their presence.

PART 1

*

A Grandparent Delights in . . .

MAGICAL MOMENTS

❦

Bill's Perspective

"Once again men and women of ripe old age will sit in the streets of Jerusalem, each with cane in hand because of his age. The city streets will be filled with boys and girls playing there."

ZECHARIAH 8:4–5

When we see seniors sharing happy moments with the young, we know that God's good hand is guiding us all.

In times of terrible trouble, the prophet Zechariah told the people of Jerusalem that God would bless them. A time would come when old people would once again sit in the streets. Children would feel free to play and enjoy the excitement of their childhood.

When you are eighteen months old, magic is all around. You explore and discover mystery as you dig in sandboxes, blow bubbles, pet kittens, and fly kites. That magic is all the more amazing if a grandparent is available to reveal the secrets of life.

One Thursday, sitting in a restaurant, I tore the paper cover off one end of a straw. Then I blew into the straw and sent the wrapper sailing across the table. Immediately I saw and heard our grandson's gleeful, wide-eyed giggle.

Beaming, I walked around the table, retrieved the paper sheath, and reloaded the straw, patiently pushing the cover back into place. Playfully, I again blew into the straw and watched the paper shoot out.

Oblivious to other patrons in the restaurant, I soon shot the paper missile straight toward the ceiling. The paper danced for a few seconds in midair and then came floating down. By this time, our grandson was ecstatic, eager to try it himself.

It was a few minutes before I wanted to give up my trick, put it in his hands. But eventually I handed over the loaded straw. He puckered his lips and blew. A misfire.

Fortunately, God sent along frosty-haired magicians and called them grandparents.

"You can do it," I said. Narrowed mouth intently fixed, he huffed and puffed. Swish! The paper cover lifted off, arched over the table, and landed quietly on a far-off chair.

We—grandparent and child—hugged each other and laughed victoriously. NASA never had a flight more successful, or important.

Parents aren't as good at magic as grandparents. Mom and Dad have important things to do. They need to do serious disciplining, keep medical records, make the child eat green mushy things, and worry about manners. Those are good things and worthy activities, and they keep most parents busy.

Parents live in a practical world. They may not have time to reload straws. They may live in fear that their child will make a fuss in a restaurant. In short, they don't have or make time for magic.

Fortunately, God sent along frosty-haired magicians and called them grandparents. They hide quarters in their hands and make them suddenly appear behind a child's ear. They make sounds like geese honking and dogs barking. Grandparents find a piece of candy in an unsuspecting child's pocket.

God has always wanted children to play in peace surrounded by people who love them. As Jeremiah 30:20 promised: "Their children will be as in days of old, and their community will be established before me."

Grandparents aren't better than parents. Children know that. But grandparents are definitely different. They have more secret compartments, more smiles, and more time to listen. At least it seems that way. There is just something magical about being a grandparent.

᥍

Lord, show me how to open new worlds to my grandchildren, providing them—and me—with magical moments.

A Grandparent Delights in . . .

MUTUAL AFFECTION

ෙ

Show me your face,
let me hear your voice;
for your voice is sweet,
and your face is lovely.
SONG OF SONGS 2:14

*A*s grandparents we're not likely to dust off old child development textbooks. Those volumes may have been great for teaching college courses, but this is the real world. The baby we now hold is someone special. This child could never be adequately explained by charts and percentages.

Understandably, parents pore over baby books and magazine articles. They quiz pediatricians and call nurses' stations. How many weeks, they want to know, before the child will grin or burp or throw up? What if he passes green stuff? If his head tilts to the left, does this mean he will be left-handed?

Frankly, we don't care if the child's finger lengths are in the top ninety-five percentile. We aren't impressed if the infant said "blah, blah" one month earlier than the national average. But don't tell the parents we feel this way. They love to match up their child and hear that he is above average. Let them enjoy it.

We grandparents play it cool. We simply know this is a perfect child.

Don't tell us that this baby can't distinguish a grandparent from the cleaning lady. Soon, and very soon at that, this infant can focus in on our eyes and smile when we pick him up and start talking. Children recognize a grandparent's extraordinary voice, the gentle tone, the excited words. Any grandparent can verify this reality.

We know that when the child smiles at us, she isn't merely passing gas. This baby holds on to Grandpa's shirt because she doesn't want Grandpa to leave. The child will quickly calm down if Grandma cuddles her and walks slowly around, humming. We know that.

We know some cries are important. Others are not. If a baby is fed and dry and keeps on crying, we put her down in her crib. If a child is healthy, a little crying never hurt. It washes out the eyes and builds strong lungs. The tears of a sick child are something else. We know that.

We try to imagine—what if a grandbaby could write? What would he say about his grandparents? It's like falling in love.

Show me your face,
    let me hear your voice;
for your voice is sweet,
    and your face is lovely.

The feeling is mutual. Our love is blind. What sheer delight.

ᔥ

Lord, thank You for these precious children and the love we share.

A Grandparent Delights in . . .

MATURING STRENGTH

✺

Pat's Perspective

And the boy Samuel continued to grow in stature and in favor with the LORD and with men.

1 SAMUEL 2:26

*O*ne of God's better gifts is seen in nature's amazing change and growth.

I put the four-month-old on his back on the floor. The next thing I knew he had rolled over onto his tummy and was scooting toward a toy.

"Look how fast you are growing!" I exclaimed.

I started mentally calculating how and where we'd get another crib for our spare room, back home. This little guy obviously couldn't be left on a bed anymore.

Growing is what children do best. Only a few months ago his parents were consumed with the needs of an infant and getting only three hours of sleep at a time.

But how quickly we noticed changes, his eyes focusing, a first coo, a smile. Before long he could be bathed in the bathtub on a spongy cushion. When he felt the warm water on his chest, his little body would relax. Soon he was kicking and laughing and splashing. And now he is eating baby foods and licking his lips at the good stuff.

Just imagine what's ahead. One day he will have a tooth poking through his gums. By Christmas he'll probably be crawling. Then someday he'll stand and take his first step. If he's like his brother, his first word will be Goose—the name of the dog.

At this stage, each time we see him, we notice how much he has changed and grown. His smile is wide and knowing.

Just wait until that first tooth gets loose. I can imagine him announcing, "Guess what, Grandma? My tooth fell out." I look forward to the day when he learns to ride a bike without training wheels. May I delight in seeing his strength and maturity as much as I did the day he first rolled over on the floor.

Planting a seed in the ground and watching it poke through the soil in the spring is good enough reason to plant a garden. But the greater joy is growing tomatoes for the children to pick and pumpkins for jack-o-lanterns.

One day our six-year-old granddaughter was kneeling down, picking green beans in our garden, when, lo and behold, a baby rabbit whooshed across her sandaled foot. Her face broke into a broad smile of shock as she felt its soft fur. She could hardly wait to phone her mother and tell about this exciting adventure.

At the birth of our first child, an older woman wisely told me: "It seems like an infant is so perfect and beautiful that you don't want him to grow up. But, trust me, a child continues to be as wonderful at every age."

These words still ring true.

ॐ

Lord, give me the spiritual ability to see the "wonderful" at every age, as my grandchildren grow up.

A Grandparent Delights in . . .

DESSERT FIRST

๑

Bill's Perspective

So I commend the enjoyment of life, because nothing is better for a man under the sun than to eat and drink and be glad. Then joy will accompany him in his work all the days of the life God has given him under the sun.

ECCLESIASTES 8:15

Celebrating food is one of the many delights handed down from grandparent to grandchild. It's a parent's job to make sure children eat spinach, oat bran, and soy. Grandparents can worry less about nutritional balance and enter into the joy of eating. A grandparent's mission is to make sure a child has more fun-food.

"When we eat with Grandpa, we get dessert first," reported our grandson who was five years old at the time. This made perfect sense to him—as it does to me. What if, heaven forbid, he stuffed himself with potatoes and meat and broccoli? Where would he then find room for ice cream, donuts, or cookies? It's too much of a risk.

Parents tend to see eating as a "problem." Maybe they should. Did the child eat on time? Did he eat his carrots? Did he have three bites of roast beef? Will treats spoil his meal? Did he take his vitamins before school, before dinner, before bed? Is his food balanced with enough good fats and not too many bad fats? Who is to argue with any of that? Children derive their eating habits at home under the careful eyes of conscientious parents. Mothers and fathers are the food police.

But the grandparent who visits occasionally and brings in some candy will never turn a child into a sugar junky. (Grandparents, of course, should be aware of allergies and diabetic concerns.)

As we see it—as grandparents—food is a celebration and not a hassle. You don't like mashed potatoes? Here, break up a brownie on top of the potatoes. Eat the whipped cream first; it will cleanse the palate. Cookies make terrific appetizers.

Our son jokingly asked his nephew at the table, "Do you want me to put the vanilla pudding in your milk?"

The lad replied excitedly, "Grandpa already did."

A grown grandson asked if he could say a few words at his grandfather's funeral. He had hundreds of warm memories from which to choose, but he focused on how often Grandpa took him to the local snack shack where they enjoyed chocolate malts.

Once in a while a grandparent needs to show up and celebrate food.

A mother complained to a grandparent, "We notice," she said, "that when you bring little Riley home, he refuses to eat the health snack we have prepared for him."

"Wow!" the grandfather replied in feigned shock. "You mean he turns down those strained peas and okra juice? What is the kid thinking?"

Once in a while a grandparent needs to show up and celebrate food. That's what God intended. Even John the Baptist slathered *honey* on his locusts. When life is good and food is plentiful, be happy. Wheat germ bread and rye dough biscuits don't always cut it. Sometimes we need to sit across the table and eat banana splits with a sparkle-eyed granddaughter.

Describing his grandparents, a child wrote, "Grandma loves Grandpa. Grandpa loves snacks."

Enjoying good food, eaten with them—it's a quality I want my grandchildren to remember about me.

৶

Lord, all good gifts come from You. Help me to enjoy those edible gifts with my grandchildren—sharing the taste, with delight.

A Grandparent Delights in . . .

TEAMWORK

❧

Pat's Perspective

For we are God's fellow workers.
1 Corinthians 3:9

*O*ne day when our three-year-old grandson was visiting, he came up with the bright idea of making a pop machine. After bringing several cardboard boxes home from the grocery store, he chose a box of the right size and his little fingers drew an eight-inch circle on the front. I cut along the lines as an opening for the pop to be dispensed.

Using colored markers, he drew a blue dot for Pepsi, a red dot for Coke, an orange dot for Slice, and a brown dot for root beer, his favorite. He then drew a line where money could be inserted; I cut a slit, and he taped a small box behind to catch the coins.

"What a fine pop machine," I bragged as I stood back and admired our craftsmanship.

But ideas were still alive in his brain.

"We need a way for the pop to roll down and come out the front," he insisted as he looked up with bright eyes.

Realizing the weight of a full can of pop, I hesitantly cautioned, "I'm not sure we can do that."

The three-year-old replied with authority, "Grandma, you can do it."

With someone believing in me that strongly, I had to press on. Together we experimented, cutting cardboard in this shape and that to design a sleeve to add to the back side. With his ideas and lots of duct tape, we did it! Our sleeve allowed pop cans to roll out flawlessly.

The machine is still in use six years later. Every time the children use it, he and I feel a sense of pride in what we accomplished together.

One Thursday our granddaughter, age five at the time, and I laid out the ingredients for poppy seed muffins. On the kitchen counter sat a large mixing bowl, mixing spoon, muffin tins, eggs, a cup of milk, and a box mix. Standing on a chair, she carefully poured in the mix and added eggs and milk and stirred. After I put the batter into the oven to bake, she sat on the floor and watched through the oven window. A delicious aroma filled the kitchen. She nearly jumped from a sitting position when the oven buzzer sounded.

After the muffins cooled, she placed them in a basket and covered them with foil. She could hardly wait till supper to serve the freshly baked muffins to her family.

Last summer, before our granddaughter came for a three-day visit, I had purchased a colorful beach towel. We chose a simple pattern to sew a beach cover-up to wear over her swim suit.

Together we measured how long it should be, cut the terry towel, pinned the sides together, and turned down the top edges. Carefully we sewed the sides. Then she put elastic through the neck opening, and we put in the finishing stitches. She was so proud of her beach cover-up that she wore it till bedtime.

Knowing the rewards of working together, I was elated to learn of the project their Sunday school undertook last winter. Each boy and girl embroidered a quilt block. Then the church women stitched them into a beautiful quilt for charity. The children felt great pride in the finished product, knowing it was their gift to others.

Teamwork—at its best it brings great joy and worthy pride. When we take the time to work alongside children, we are teaching them to solve problems and modeling life skills. Ultimately teamwork multiplies what we can do alone, for the family, for the community, or for the kingdom of God.

ॐ

Lord, thank You for the joy of working together, with our grandchildren, with others in the church and community, and with You.

A Grandparent Delights in . . .

HAVING FUN

❦

Bill's Perspective

*"He will yet fill your mouth with laughter
and your lips with shouts of joy."*

JOB 8:21

*T*his statement was made by Bildad to Job. I'm not sure what all Bildad had in mind, but I do know that later Job became a grandparent. He saw his children and their children into the fourth generation. This alone should have given him great reason to laugh and skip and push swings and engage in slush battles.

Today—Thursday—we had slush battles in the park.

Each of us got an icy slush; choose any flavor. Then someone said (oh, it wasn't me, was it?), "Look at those clouds. It must be going to rain."

As the grandchildren peered into the bright sky, I drew in a strawful of colored ice and spewed it all over their unsuspecting heads.

Surprised by their grandfather's attack, each child quickly got to his own straw. Soon they were running in circles, blasting one another with flying chipped ice. All in fun, of course.

If God allows us to live long enough to see our grandchildren (and sometimes that doesn't take too long), then we could experience a whole new set of joys and satisfactions.

Aging is more than fallen arches and plastic partials. It's also an opportunity to spread happiness into the lives of children. And they into ours.

We all admire the virtuous woman of Proverbs 31. Verse 25 says that she can "laugh at the days to come." Maybe she was dreaming of grandchildren and the mischievous things they might do.

Wait a minute. Who's instigating the mischief?

No, you don't say.

⑤

Lord, may I be courageous enough to let loose and have fun with my grandchildren.

A Grandparent Delights in ...

CELEBRATORY EVENTS

✧

Pat's Perspective

"Suppose a woman has ten silver coins and loses one. ... And when she finds it, she calls her friends and neighbors together and says, 'Rejoice with me; I have found my lost coin.'"

LUKE 15:8–9

*D*o you remember the Mary Poppins song, "Every day's a holiday with [you, dear]"? This may be true concerning our grandchildren, but sometimes with a little effort and planning, we can make an event of it.

Every year we try to schedule a summer festival in our driveway and invite all the grandkids and their families. Bill dresses up as the Water Festival Man. (No one is supposed to know who he really is.)

He wears a goofy umbrella hat, shorts, and no shoes. He carries a box filled with water balloons. The festivities begin with an adults-only egg toss, spouses matched as teams. The children love to watch their parents play this game.

After everyone has a crack at the egg toss (get it?), we turn to the water balloons. No one escapes from the tossing and smashing. We aren't satisfied until everyone is totally soaked—and laughing.

After several hours of fun, the Water Festival Man disappears. Throughout the year, the grandchildren ask when he is going to return.

Traditional holidays make good celebrations, but it certainly is acceptable to declare a few extra ones. Once in a while we announce a half-birthday. On a Thursday, we take the grandchildren to a bakery and order a small cake, which we cut up and eat in the snack area. It's too hard to wait a whole year to enjoy birthdays.

Traditional holidays make good celebrations, but it certainly is acceptable to declare a few extra ones.

Then there was the Chocolate Festival. We invited everyone over and served thirty different kinds of chocolate. They ate for forty minutes. Anything they wanted. It takes great parents to go along with that one.

Grandparents are limited only by their imaginations. Life holds enough hard times. Look for events to celebrate: summer, winter, spring, fall, tooth loss, graduation to a new grade, a child memorizing Psalm 23. Not every day, but often enough to break the routine and mark the good.

ᔐ

Lord, give us eyes to see reasons to celebrate new holidays, annually or just one time.

A Grandparent Delights in . . .

A SHARED BELIEF

$$\circledS$$

Bill's Perspective

[Timothy,] I know that you sincerely trust the Lord, for you have the faith of your mother, Eunice, and your grandmother, Lois.

2 TIMOTHY 1:5 NLT

*T*he large prairie on the edge of town stretches out over meadows and forests and ponds. My grandson and I have been on the park trail many times over the past nine years. At first, when he was about three years old, he was reluctant to go, but by now he has memorized the points of interest. We take the guidebook along, but neither of us needs it.

There are cottonwoods along the path. Around the bend we can pick up handfuls of coffeetree pods. At the pond, ducks swoop in, slam on their brakes, and settle down on the water. Over the hill we see buffalo or bison, shoulders large and strong. A little further on, there is an antelope with majestic antlers. This isn't an amusement park with roller coasters and bumper cars, but it has its own sense of wonder. Over and over again.

Each visit leaves a clear impression on our memories. Beavers in the ponds, snakes along the path, bees flying in and out of the nature house. Then there was a special day. . . .

Walking across the bridge, we saw a fence post. And on that post there was . . . a huge, mostly black bird. Only a few feet away from us sat a turkey vulture, its body about two feet long. My grandson and I stopped cold. Excited and amazed. Being observers, not hunters, we stood silently, hoping not to scare it away. We stepped closer. It turned its red head toward us. It seemed more curious than concerned. Finally, after a few minutes, it stretched its wide wings; with two slow, long flaps, it took off. Several yards away it slowly landed again on another post.

"I bet it escaped from the cages further into the park," I ventured.

My grandson nodded silently, and we continued, contentedly, on our way.

When we arrived home that evening, he told his parents what we had seen, then added, "We believe it must live in one of the cages. That's why it was so calm."

I was surprised to hear my own words coming from the young man. "We believe . . . ," he had said.

That's right, I thought. We had spent the day together, and "we" both believed the same thing. We hadn't passed the day discussing philosophy or theology. And yet the values and beliefs I owned were being dispersed; effortlessly my grandson was gathering them in. School had been in session and yet no bells had rung. Information was being exchanged without chalkboards or computers. Faith was being shared without pulpits or pews.

The values and beliefs I owned were being dispersed; effortlessly my grandson was gathering them in.

Christian faith comes from God, but it usually enters life through one or many human vehicles: a minister, a witness, a teacher, a caring parent. In 2 Timothy the apostle Paul says that the young man Timothy shared the faith of his grandmother Lois.

If I was so pleased that my grandson and I shared an opinion about a bird's habitat, I can hardly imagine Lois's delight at knowing that Timothy shared her belief in the Lord Jesus Christ.

ᔓ

Lord, thank You that my grandchildren and I together can learn about Your creation and You personally.

PART 2

❧

From Grandchildren
a Grandparent Can Learn . . .

TO RUN THE RACE

Bill's Perspective

Let us run with perseverance the race marked out for us.

HEBREWS 12:1

A two-year-old boy has put running back into this senior citizen's life. I used to enjoy running, but recently my exercise has become a measured walk. If you tell the energetic toddler we are going for a milkshake, you'd better have your sneakers already tied.

He races down the walkway, makes a hard left and keeps going. The snack place is four blocks away from our house, and he will run every inch of the distance. A heavy-breathing grandfather's only chance of keeping up is long legs.

Life is too interesting to be wasted sitting around taking a nap. There are places to go, things to see, stuff to do.

As grandchildren run, they are also preparing to run the race of life. Not a race measured by speed alone, but more accurately by the godly wisdom they collect along the way. They will learn right and wrong, righteousness and evil, and they will be able to run wisely.

I guide you in the way of wisdom
and lead you along straight paths.

When you walk, your steps will not be hampered;
when you run, you will not stumble.

PROVERBS 4:11–12

Beaches are wide-open spaces. This same grandchild sees them as perfect running grounds on an early morning just after breakfast. He was born to run.

Jogging just a few paces behind him, I realize how good life can be. At retirement age my first impulse would have been to stroll pensively, arms behind my back. Fortunately, this child isn't into beard-stroking. And because of him I'm pounding my shoes into the sandy shoreline.

The race may be just beginning for him, but I am reminded that it continues on for me. Jesus Christ still has purpose for me. My heavenly Father doesn't consider me too old.

With freedom and freshness, I run along. Head up high, wind in my face, a new spring in my step. My young running instructor leads me on to new challenges.

The race is on for both of us.

🌀

Lord, at any age, may we run the race of life with integrity.

From Grandchildren a Grandparent Can Learn . . .

A POSITIVE PERSPECTIVE

๖

Pat's Perspective

My heart is steadfast, O God. . . .
With God we will gain the victory.

PSALM 108:1, 13

*I*t was our daughter and son-in-law's tenth wedding anniversary, and their family had stopped to overnight with us on their way to a get-away celebration.

The children had gone to sleep easily that night. But at 5:15 A.M. I heard my two-year-old grandson calling, "Mama!"

I rose to the occasion. I rubbed his back. Then I picked him up, held him, and sang for a while to help him go back to sleep. But the train whistle and Grandpa's snoring guaranteed that he was awake for the day.

Oh, good, I thought. *Just the two of us can go downstairs while the rest of the family sleeps. We will have some fun time alone.*

So down the stairs we walked, oh so quietly. As I turned on a light, the little guy shrieked, "A bird in da house!"

A winged creature suddenly swooped through the hallway. Telling my grandson to stay back, I flung the front door wide open. Shoo. Shoo. Fly out. But the varmint had other ideas. It zipped back and forth from one end of the living room to the other, nowhere near the doorway.

My grandson was thrilled. He danced back and forth clapping and singing, "Bird, go out! Bird, go out!"

Bird? It was a *bat*.

Grabbing a pillow from the couch, I whooshed at the furry fiend each time it came toward me.

"Bird, go out!" sang a little voice from the hallway. He was having a wonderful time.

I dashed for the broom and swung it with all my might. With one gigantic heave, I knocked the bat to the floor, quickly smothered it with an afghan, and gathered up the corners. In an instant the bat was thrown out the door.

While the rest of the family slept peacefully, my grandson and I ate a big breakfast, played trains, and at daylight went out to the sandbox in our pajamas.

Throughout the entire day, my grandson told everyone he saw, "Gwamma knock bird down. Frow'd him out."

What I experienced as a stressful encounter, a two-year-old saw as adventure—with me as the heroine. May I learn from him—to ratchet down the stress level when I'm upset when the furnace goes out on a cold night, when our plans get scrapped because of something out of our control. May I face the situation with a positive outlook, anticipating adventure. Who knows what tales I'll be able to tell anyone who will listen.

ॶ

Lord, give me grace to see the stresses that dart into my life as adventures, and in those adventures, allow my grandchildren to see me as their hero.

KINGDOM CHILDHOOD

§

Bill's Perspective

"Unless you change and become like little children, you will never enter the kingdom of heaven. Therefore, whoever humbles himself like this child is the greatest in the kingdom of heaven."

MATTHEW 18:3

*S*ome goal-oriented grandparents want to teach their grandchildren to read, count, and run computers. I set my sights a little lower. I taught our grandson to ride elevators. Fifteen years from now this probably won't help on his SAT test. His fifth-grade teacher isn't likely to call his mother and breathlessly ask, "Did you know your son can ride elevators?" It doesn't even sound good on my headstone: "He Taught His Grandchildren the Ups and Downs of Life."

But then, that isn't why this two-year-old and I started this practice. One day I asked if he wanted to push the button, and for the next two years we rode practically every elevator in the city. Many times.

Of all the elevators we rode, in restaurants, office buildings, and the state capitol, certainly the best were at the local hospital. There are banks of elevators. Four on a side. You can bounce in and out like a city subway. Sometimes it was just the two of us and other times there were twelve. You have to learn to stay cool, push buttons, and look like you belong there. He was a master at it. Especially once he learned not to hop on the elevator and immediately push all ten buttons.

In our riding years, he may have learned a little bit about cause and effect. Possibly he learned something about power and a smidgen about safety. But those weren't the goals. My first goal was to spend time with him, for his sake. I want him to grow up feeling that he is special enough and worthwhile enough for someone to want to be with him. He won't recall the day when we sat on the ledge outside one building and argued over what to do next. More elevator rides? (His idea.) Or was it time to move on? (My idea.) The preschooler cried, and my eyes welled up. Then he looked at me and said, "Grandpa, I love you." He won't remember that exchange, though I hope he will always feel the love behind those tears.

If I want to study theology, I am told to study children. Is that strange or what?

As for me—I'll never forget that day, which brings me to my second goal: to spend time with him, for my sake, to learn what it means to be childlike. If we hold a relentless grip on our adulthood and deny our childhood, we will miss some important aspects of our faith. Funny how that works. If I want to study theology, I am told to study children. Is that strange or what?

By spending time with children, I can get a clearer view and understanding of what Jesus called the "kingdom of heaven." I don't have to teach preschool to learn these lessons, though I could. Instead, God gave me grandchildren, and in their presence I can learn to understand and experience the wide-eyed wonder, the curiosity, the humility, the love, and the trust that all together begins to define the kingdom of heaven.

⑤

Heavenly Father, as I spend time with the grandchildren I love, show me what Your kingdom is all about.

From Grandchildren a Grandparent Can Learn . . .

TO CONSIDER THE FLOWERS

❧

Pat's Perspective

"Consider the lilies of the field."
MATTHEW 6:28 KJV

When you are a year-and-a-half old, everything on the ground is an adventure. Ants, caterpillars, candy wrappers, flowers—it doesn't make much difference. And when you and your small grandchild go for a walk, no one needs to be in a hurry.

One morning when I was walking with my grandson, he stopped to pick some dandelions. As everyone knows, a slippery-stemmed dandelion cannot be picked quickly. Small fingers have trouble learning this new skill. Sometimes the flowers slide right through the toddler's fingers. Again and again and again, and then the stemmed flower wondrously pulls loose.

After a good while he held three beautiful buds. Then he dropped one and had to pick it up. That took a bit of time. Soon he dropped a second one. I waited while his untrained hand secured that one too.

The average adult might find this exercise tedious. He or she would be tempted to scoop up the flowers and hurry the little horticulturist along. But grandparents aren't average adults. When we hang out with grandchildren, it's as if we are going to school.

This warm summer day was perfect for heading to the school playground. Up and down the play structure, over and under the tunnels.

And from this vantage point we could watch the trains go by. He is the train-loving child. Hearing a train whistle in the distance, he stopped suddenly and said, "Choo-Choo." Hand in hand we raced toward the tracks and sat down on the ground, waiting. Soon the behemoth rolled into sight, and the toddler sat motionless as it passed by, 130 cars filled with coal.

Then a wide puddle caught his eye, fresh rain water from the previous night having settled on the school driveway. Quick as a flash he headed toward it. We took off our shoes and waded together, laughing with delight.

As we proceeded on our happy adventure, there were wood chips, pine-cones, tiny purple wildflowers, bark in a multitude of shapes, smooth pebbles, blades of grass, sandy patches, tiny and big leaves.

I cherish the memory of this summer morning, as we walked and played together but also walked with God, touching parts of His creation, considering the lilies, or at least the dandelions and the pinecones and tree leaves.

෯

Lord, thank You for a chance to slow down and notice Your marvelous world.

TO WEEP WITH THOSE WHO WEEP

❧

Pat's Perspective

Mourn with those who mourn.

ROMANS 12:15

At the end of our delightful afternoon at the fair, we were all happy, but hot and tired and ready to head home.

Our six-year-old granddaughter had been especially interested in the kind, old clown at the Jaycee booth. He was a balloon artist. She had stood close and watched intently as he pulled a long balloon from his raggedy coat pocket.

"Young lady, would you like a bunny?" he asked.

He dazzled her with his deft movements as he blew into the balloon enough air to make a head of a bunny. Then he skillfully pinched it to form long ears; he blew and twisted just so, to make a fat tummy and legs and a round tail. The smiling clown laughed and joked all the while.

When he presented the pink bunny to her, she was as happy as she would be if Christmas arrived in July. Thanking him with a high-five clap, she skipped back to us holding her bunny gently.

All the way home she played with it, planning to show it to her mom. This was a treasure, which the clown had made especially for her.

As we piled out of the car, Balloon Bunny somehow snagged on the door or touched the hot exterior of the car. And poof! Bunny was gone. Our little granddaughter, who does not often cry, burst into tears, holding the remains of what had been her cherished bunny. She had owned many balloons before, but this one was special. Her heart was broken.

No big deal, I thought. *Surely, at six years old, she knows that balloons do not last. She'll soon have supper and will feel better.*

We hurried all the children inside and prepared to leave.

Fortunately, Mommy immediately saw the sadness in her daughter's face and held her close; she listened and talked soothingly to her.

We debriefed the wonderful time we had had, said our good-byes, and were out the door.

Then, on the way to our house, it hit me. Maybe a balloon is a small thing, one of a myriad of disappointments. But . . . I knew I had been uncaring. It would have meant a lot to our granddaughter if I had just stopped to be with her in her pain.

My lack of tenderness bothered me all evening.

The next morning I phoned our daughter and immediately asked to speak to the six-year-old.

"I just wanted to call and tell you that I'm so sorry your bunny balloon burst yesterday."

"Oh, that's OK," she said brightly. "I took the rest of the balloon and made a snake."

She was OK now. But, also, I was assured that "we" were OK. We were still buddies. A friendship requires understanding and caring. Next time, may I be more sensitive to knowing when a loss, though small, should be acknowledged, not shrugged off.

§

Lord, give me a heart that knows when to weep with those who weep—even with little people, even for little losses.

TO REJOICE WITH THOSE WHO REJOICE

⟨S⟩

Bill's Perspective

Rejoice with those who rejoice.
ROMANS 12:15

*M*y job was to find trains. That was evident from the time he was only a year old. Coal trains run six blocks from our house, and the minute our grandson arrives, the assignment is clear: "Choo-Choos," he shouts and points. "Choo-Choos."

Barely walking, he would toddle down the street with boundless energy. The little guy could walk anywhere, anytime, to see an engine and a caboose. A caboose was any part of the train that wasn't an engine.

On other occasions we would get in the car and drive for miles looking for trains. One time we saw a couple of engines sitting idle, so we drove up close and parked. I put my happy grandson on the roof of our car and we watched.

In a few minutes an engineer climbed inside one of the huge orange engines. Without warning, he blasted the whistle. My grandson was so startled, he jumped into the air from a sitting position and shouted with joy. The engineer then stuck his head and arm out the window and gave a wide exaggerated wave. We waved back, shouted, and clapped our hands.

As the train pulled out of the yard, grandson and grandfather laughed together, totally thrilled at the kindness of that generous engineer.

That's what we have learned to expect from hanging out with little children. Joy comes their way, and it spills over into our lives, too.

One day our daughter left a message on the answering machine followed by the voice of a small two-year-old shouting with gladness, "I go potty!"

That may not sound like earth-shaking news, but every grandparent knows what a big deal it is. This tiny tyke had just reached a milestone, and he wanted to share the news with people who were special to him.

That was better news than the stock market going up a hundred points.

As with other communication, joy needs two components. It needs a sender and a receiver. A grandchild will have many reasons to sound out gladness and joy. He or she will be looking for a special someone to send it to. Fortunate is the grandparent who is in the right place to hear it.

Blessed is the person who answers the phone and hears a little voice saying loudly, "I go potty."

It's time to rejoice with those who rejoice.

ᔕ

Lord, I want to be in touch with my grandchildren, so I can rejoice with them in their happiness.

From Grandchildren a Grandparent Can Learn...

THE MEANING OF TRUST

Bill's Perspective

*Trust in the LORD with all your heart
and lean not on your own understanding.*

PROVERBS 3:5

$\mathcal{M}$y grandson was nine years old. It seemed the perfect age for him to visit Washington, D.C., with me as his companion and guardian. I grew up in the nation's capital and looked forward to this special return with my grandson.

Catching a plane to D.C. was still a nerve-racking situation when we went, after the hijackings in September 2001, but I determined not to frighten my grandson. No doubt everything would go well. Why should I create apprehension?

However, the flying experience was not without its cautions, set in place by people other than me. When we boarded our plane in Nebraska, security was tight. Our baggage was checked electronically. We took off our shoes and placed them on the conveyor belt. My grandson had nothing in his pockets, but I had to unload everything from mine into the plastic basket.

Trusting all the way, my grandson followed instructions more with curiosity than with fear.

The two-and-one-half-hour plane ride was uneventful until we approached Washington. Then the pilot got on the mike: "Listen up. During the final thirty minutes of flight no one will be allowed to get out of his or her seat for any reason. No one must use the restroom. If anyone stands up, the plane will automatically divert to another airport."

My grandson didn't bat an eyelash. Flying into Baltimore or Philadelphia would just be an extra story to tell. Besides, if anything went wrong, well, Grandpa could handle it.

How relieved I felt when we landed without incident. Right at the airport we jumped onto the subway, which got us near enough to anywhere we wanted to be, anything we wanted to see, for five days.

After exploring the great city, with its many museums and monuments, we packed our bags to return home. The night before our flight, while my grandson was sleeping, I heard a news report: Security at Reagan National Airport might be on high alert the next day; there was a potential threat of terrorism. I decided not to warn the boy that anything might be different than on our previous flight.

At the airport, check-in went smoothly. We saw no evidence of military police. We weren't frisked by security officers, though my belt buckle made the machine buzz. Once on the plane, we buckled in, ordered a meal, and took out books to read. The pilot announced, "If anyone stands up, for any reason, during the first thirty minutes of flight, our plane will divert to another airport."

I saw trust up close. My grandson became my object lesson.

My grandson gave another innocent, trusting smile. Stopping off in Philadelphia still sounded good to him.

He had little idea what all the dangers might be. As the plane taxied on the tarmac, he didn't know there was at least one loaded pistol on the plane. One of these ordinary-guy passengers was a U.S. marshal, alert and prepared to take control.

Snuggled into our seats, I was impressed with how much he trusted me as his guardian. If Grandpa was on the plane with him, it must be all right. Grandpa would take care of him.

On that trip I saw trust up close. My grandson became my object lesson. Seeing the trust of a child makes it easier for me, and maybe you, to trust in the Lord. He is with us. And He is trustworthy.

ᔕ

Lord, we relax in Your care. Thank You for being our loving heavenly Father.

PART 3

🌀

From Grandchildren
A Grandparent Receives . . .

From Grandchildren a Grandparent Receives . . .

A CROWN OF HONOR

⚛

Bill's Perspective

Children's children are a crown to the aged.

*I*t takes loving parents to trust grandparents with their children. After all, we raised children thirty years ago, before disposable diapers, baby monitors, and pills to address every sneeze and twitch. How can we know how to care for children? We didn't even take the breathing classes.

One summer evening I took an infant grandchild out for a walk. I did the walking; the baby cuddled close in the crook of my arm. It's hard to beat good physical contact.

About dusk, I headed back toward the parents' home. Soon, a man walking his dog called out to me.

"Oh, you must be the one they're looking for."

Looking for me? Do they think I'm senile? Do they think I'm at the park talking to trash cans?

"Oh, yeah," he continued, "a young man is driving around the neighborhood asking if we've seen an old guy carrying a baby."

Now I was mumbling to myself.

Arriving at their house I saw the young parents standing by their car, trying to appear relaxed. I walked directly to them and said matter-of-factly, "I don't know what's wrong with me this evening. I keep dropping the baby." (Don't try this line unless everyone has a sense of humor.)

Children don't have to have two generations to raise them, but it can't hurt. The parents are there to worry. Grandparents are there to accept, praise, and buy maple-covered donuts.

Parents work day and night to make the children perfect. Grandparents believe the children are already perfect; all they really need is someone to run along beside them.

Parents wring their hands and plan for tomorrow. Grandparents close their eyes and fall asleep remembering how wonderful today was.

Parents ought to have wrinkled brows. Grandparents ought not. (Custodial grandparents are in a different category.)

As visiting grandparents, our job description is to carry grandchildren around on our shoulders so they can see the parade. We get them extra tickets at the county fair, where Grandma goes with them on the death-defying octopus ride. We let them stay up late, sleep in late, and just be late if it suits them.

As I see it, that's the way God intended it. Grandchildren aren't products we mold. The book of Proverbs says they are crowns that we wear.

God crowned me a grandparent. I'd say that's something similar to being knighted without the formality. Something like being a guardian angel but far more visible.

When a grandfather walks to the park, holding hands with a pint-sized three-year-old, he wears a crown of honor more precious than gold.

Lord, help me to be a grandparent who is worthy of such a crown of honor.

From Grandchildren a Grandparent Receives...

RESTORED RELATIONSHIPS

🌀

*"He will turn the hearts of the fathers to their children,
and the hearts of the children to their fathers."*

MALACHI 4:6

Suppose you and your daughter didn't get along well during her turbulent adolescent years. Let's just pretend that you heard a few careless comments such as, "Nobody loves me around here." Or the stabbing line, "I hate you." Or the too-familiar announcement: "I'll be glad when I don't live here anymore."

More parents have heard more outrageous statements like these than we want to admit. So much for words. What about the actions? Breaking curfews, using booze, taking the car without permission. . . . If our children are grown, we aren't anxious to drag all of that out again.

Let's go to the good news. When our children have children, a redemptive process goes into motion. If we let it.

Even the harshest, most fractured parent-child relationship can leap a generation and blossom into a healthy grandparent-grandchild connection. The birth of a child can bring hope, happiness, and forgiveness into a bristling relationship.

If nothing else, our children are far more likely to tolerate us when they see how much we love their babies. The fact that we didn't buy him the red sports car when he was a teen, the fact that she once dated the town goon . . . no longer seems important.

Too many parents stay away from their grandchild because they still can't handle their rude child or her greasy significant other. What a sad waste. The grand-baby arrives as a peace offering, whether anyone realizes it or not.

God has a habit of bringing redemption through children: Baby Moses to free a nation, Baby John the Baptist to lead the way . . . for Baby Jesus to redeem humankind. And now Baby Con-nor or Baby Emily to build a bridge, soften hearts, and draw three generations together.

The birth of a child can bring hope, happiness, and forgive-ness into a bristling relationship.

If you found a child in a snowbank on a cold winter's night, you would pick it up. Who could walk away and hope the baby would disappear?

God sent a baby into your family. You pick it up, look into those bright eyes, and notice the dimple in his cheek.

Children can lead the way to restore relationships across generations. All we have to do is give them a chance.

๑

Lord, thank You for bringing healing and restoration into our lives.

From Grandchildren a Grandparent Receives...

SATISFACTION

❦

Pat's Perspective

"If you then, though you are evil, know how to give good gifts to your children, how much more will your Father in heaven give the Holy Spirit to those who ask him!"
LUKE 11:13

*T*he circus was coming to the downtown arena. For weeks ahead we watched the newspaper to find the date. None of us had ever been. Books and movies had shown the wonders of a circus, but I had waited for sixty years to see it live.

We didn't tell the grandchildren until the day before, trying to prevent impatient daily early-morning questions: "Is this the day? Is this the day?"

When our daughter told them, "Tomorrow Grandpa and Grandma are taking you to the circus," for a moment they all sat silent, drinking in what their mom had just said. One can only imagine what was racing through their minds. It was *the* topic of conversation for the next twenty-four hours.

Finally Circus Thursday arrived. When we stopped to pick them up, the children were dressed and ready. You'd think we were going to meet the president. They sported their best shirts and hair ribbons.

As we drove across town, anticipation ran high as we talked about tigers, elephants, flying trapezes, men shot from cannons.... "Grandpa," blurted our four-year-old granddaughter, "will you buy me cotton candy?" She'd seen but never tasted the sweet-swirled wonder. Did it taste as good as it looked? She was very curious.

Would Grandpa buy her cotton candy? *Honey,* he thought, *if I have to mortgage the house, you'll get cotton candy.*

As we parked, we heard calliope music and saw clowns with straggly red hair waving balloons. Bill and I held each child's hand as we walked into the arena and climbed up the steps to Row W.

Soon the band played and the ringmaster ran to the center ring. Let the show begin!

There was so much to see: Ponies pranced in one ring, while overhead an acrobat walked a high wire. We all laughed at a rickety Model T backfiring and bouncing around, then we held our breath as lions jumped through a fire ring. A motorcycle zoomed through the air.

And, yes, we had cotton candy.

Seeing those lions and tigers and bears perform for the first time didn't compare with the satisfaction I received watching a child taste her first swirl of cotton candy.

As she crawled into bed that night, the little cotton-candy lover told her dad, "When I grow up, I want to be in the circus." The next day she donned her boots and a high hat, used a ruler for a baton, and "directed" her stuffed animals, strategically positioned around the living room in her pretend circus.

I can only imagine that the satisfaction I sensed as her grandpa met a child's small request must be multiplied thousands of times for God when we turn to Him and ask for the Spirit's guidance and help in our lives. He is eager to give. He delights in giving good gifts.

ᔕ

Lord, thank You for being the giver of all good gifts.

"NEWNESS"

§

Because of the LORD's great love we are not consumed,
for his compassions never fail. They are new every
morning; great is your faithfulness.

LAMENTATIONS 3:22–23

One Thursday afternoon we—two adults and three children—sat in a theater munching popcorn, sipping sodas. We were watching—for the third time—the most popular children's animated movie ever produced.

What a great story line. A father-fish fights against impossible odds to rescue his son-fish. Magnificent colors. Excellent music. Beautiful artwork. It's all there.

But what are the odds that we would have been there if we didn't have grandchildren? Children simply refuse to let us grow old quickly. Their energy calls us away from our hobbies, away from our overstuffed chairs, and into the exciting world of today.

Without grandchildren we would seldom venture into the mysteries of a computer. Children are the only reason we go bowling. Why else would we play tag and chase each other around the yard? (We never do that when they aren't around; trust me.)

We have climbed through space labs and ridden Ferris wheels. We have dug sand tunnels by the ocean, sung lustily in the car, and played video games. We have enjoyed all these activities—when it would have been easier to take a nap.

Far from spectators, grandparents are called on to go places and do things. We swim in the heat of the day, hike on the nearest nature trail, and participate at science fairs. (And we thought grandparents were supposed to raise violets and feed cats.)

If we had not connected with our grandchildren, we would have missed all of this—what shall we call it?—newness. Our best years would have been behind us, in the past. We would have missed setting up train tracks on the living room floor, racing traction cars in the dining room, and playing team chess. We would have missed new books, new authors, and new films.

If we had not connected with our grandchildren, we would have missed all of this—what shall we call it?— newness.

The problem with some older people is not that they remember so many old things, but that all they know is old things. Grandchildren give us an added respect for the new. Because of them, we know that many new things are amazing.

God doesn't fall into that trap. His greatest years are not in the past. Much of His good work is yet to come. If we search the Scriptures for how often God deals in the "new," we gain appreciation for how fresh and far-reaching it is.

Each day is new, and much of what it brings is new, too. Grandparents get up and greet the newness. Sometimes it comes through the lives of children who bless our lives. Often the newness comes from the hands of a here-and-now God.

ᘓ

Lord, whose mercies are new every morning, bring the delight of "newness" into my heart today.

From Grandchildren a Grandparent Receives . . .

LATTER-DAY BLESSINGS

෧

Bill's Perspective

The LORD blessed the latter part of Job's life more than the first. . . .

After this, Job lived a hundred and forty years; he saw his children and their children to the fourth generation. And so he died, old and full of years.

JOB 42:12, 16–17

I've never been comfortable discussing blessings or rewards. I certainly don't deserve any. None! But the Bible says God gives them to me anyway. And some of those blessings are grandchildren. Fortunately, I've had the opportunity to cash in a few of those coupons while I'm still on earth.

Like the five days I spent with my grandson in Washington, D.C. What were we doing in D.C.? A sixty-five-year-old and a nine-year-old grandson checking out the seat of government? I was collecting some of my rewards.

The National Geographic Society and the "money factory" at the Bureau of Engraving were probably his favorite sites.

At the National Air and Space Museum, we saw a laboratory where astronauts work in space. We looked down on the city from the top of the Washington Monument. We walked the halls of the Capitol. The tour of the Library of Congress was a kick for a kid who loves libraries. Imagine—450 miles of bookshelves!

As an extra bonus, we heard, then saw in the sky, two helicopters with the presidential seal. Which one carried the president? I guess one never knows.

There was more to see than we could take in. For all the history and museums at hand, I was amazed that my grandson took such an interest in the subway, of all things. He loved the maps and the fare machines that spit out cards faster than I could think. Who can predict just what rings another person's bell?

Standing under a tree, near the Capitol, we laughed, joked, and got soaked in an afternoon rain. Glasses fogged over, socks wringing wet, I collected all the blessings I could handle.

Who knows if Job ever stood under a tree with his grandchildren and laughed in the pouring rain. But he could have. Because God blessed his life.

A savings account is important, and I dabble in preparing for the future. But when it comes to grandchildren, I want to cash in now. God gave us gifts we don't deserve, and I have decided to go ahead and use them while I can.

Being with grandchildren is accepting my blessings from the Lord.

⑤

Lord, my heart overflows with thanks to You for the blessings You give me in these latter years of my life.

A SECOND YOUTH

⟡

Bill's Perspective

*[God] satisfies [my] desires with good things,
so that [my] youth is renewed like the eagle's.*
PSALM 103:5

The Naomi of the Old Testament had many disappointments. She felt the heavy burden of losing people she loved; her husband and two sons had died.

After some time her daughter-in-law Ruth remarried and gave birth to a child. Because of Jewish law, this boy became Naomi's grandson. The New Living Translation of Ruth 4:15 notes a blessing given to Naomi: "May this child restore your youth."

Anyone who has actively grandparented knows that grandchildren have an energizing and life-giving power.

Why did God send a grandchild your way? Why did He place innocence, love, gentleness, and joy into your life at this stage? For many reasons, but none is more important than this: The Lord knew it would restore your youth and vitality.

The Lord sent the fountain of youth and wrapped it in a diaper. A grandchild is new blood to aging bones. A fresh spirit to a sagging attitude. Grandchildren restore our sense of belonging, our sense of purpose, and our sense of hope. This tiny bundle lets you know someone wants you, needs you, and accepts you exactly as you are. An infant's smile tells us she wants to connect with someone who is willing to be part of her life.

But it's not all about infants. Grandparents who get involved with children are less likely to sit and rust out; they are busy hiking trails, carving pumpkins, and buying bicycle helmets. They have the same arthritic knees as the other seniors, but they don't seem to notice it as much.

Someone said the goal of life is to die young as late as possible. Few opportunities give us as much youth as entering the world of children. Chasing balls, making up stories, building model cars, tossing water balloons are all acts of defiance. We are fighting off the effects of aging.

Last Thursday we decided to take the grandchildren to a water park. That's the best place to be in July heat. *While the children frolic on the waterslide and jump off the boards,* I told myself, *I can nap on a lounge chair or maybe read a book.*

The Lord sent the fountain of youth and wrapped it in a diaper.

Before long I was in the pool, swimming like a shark, picking up children, and tossing them high into the air. We hugged, laughed, raced, and splashed. Later we sat at a table by the concession stand, drank pop, ate ice cream sandwiches, and told stories.

There is nothing like children to ruin an old guy's nap. Even so, I drove the kids back home, remembering the words of my wife: "Oh, they do a lot more for me than I ever do for them." I knew my grandkids gave me a second crack at youth.

⑨

Lord, thank You for these young lives and how they spread anticipation, joy, and gladness.

PART 4

🌀

A Wise Grandparent Knows . . .

THE PRIVILEGE OF MAKING DECISIONS

٩

Bill's Perspective

"Choose for yourselves this day whom you will serve. . . . But as for me and my household, we will serve the LORD."

JOSHUA 24:15

One Thursday morning, as soon as my grandson and I were buckled up in the car, I turned and asked, "How do you like it best? Do you want me to plan these outings and tell you what we are going to do, or would you rather choose?"

"I'd rather choose," he replied.

That takes the pressure off. There is no need to become the grandchild's entertainment director and desperately hope he enjoys it. Throwing out ideas and allowing him to decide makes it more fun for everyone.

Before my first grandson could write, we began our Thursdays together by making lists of what we might do. We ate breakfast once a week in the same McDonald's for almost eight years. While we ate pancakes, scrambled eggs, sausage, and biscuits and jelly, we drew pictures, created new planets, and imagined new continents. Then on a paper napkin we listed where we might go for the next hour or two.

For each suggestion I made, he drew a simple picture. Do we want to ride elevators? He drew an elevator. How about the state capitol? Want to check out the park? We haven't been to the bookstore or the library lately. He drew as many as a dozen pictures. What was the hurry? Talking, eating, drawing, choosing, these were as much fun as going places. After all, this was no big production. As you might guess, usually the simplest hours were the happiest.

List completed, we then chose three top-rated places. Off we went to see how many we could take in. If we got to only one, it made no difference.

To be sure, a few times I announced that we were going to a preplanned place. That's how we created new adventures. But mostly we took the time to stretch our minds together and explore the possibilities. This is how any of us expands the pleasure of decision-making.

God gave us humans the privilege of making decisions. He didn't have to, but He did. Even young children are capable of making small decisions. To do so, they need information (clearly stated options from which to choose) and opportunity or permission to make a selection.

God gave us humans the privilege of making decisions.

Pat and I don't spend time with the grandchildren because we want to teach them truths. Almost all the teaching goes on as a side benefit, including this life-lesson in decision-making. You see, in time, the big spiritual decisions are better weighed by those who aren't afraid to make decisions. As grandchildren grow, they can *choose* to serve the Lord, because they have experienced making small choices. Part of their preparation is having adults who respect them and give them options.

What shall we do today, go to the park or play in the back-yard?

§

Lord, help me—and my grandchildren as they grow—make decisions that bless others and please You.

WHEN TO STAY SILENT

☙

Bill's Perspective

When words are many, sin is not absent,
but he who holds his tongue is wise.
PROVERBS 10:19

*T*he Bible teaches me to watch what I say, but it isn't an easy lesson. When I think I have so much wisdom, I am eager to pass it on to my children and their spouses. The trick is to know when to bite my tongue. Which is often.

A noted psychologist writes a column that appears regularly in our newspaper. He discusses everything from toilet training to disciplining to eating habits. Frequently he writes on topics that I believe our children need to know about.

Occasionally I plan to leave the paper out on their kitchen counter. What could be wrong with a subtle hint to guide them along life's parenting highway? Or I contemplate clipping out a column and mailing it. Everybody likes to receive mail, I figure.

Thankfully, I've never carried out either plan. I know how it would be received. Our children would consider this an interference or criticism. And they would be right.

The book of Proverbs gives me a strong clue:

A man of understanding holds his tongue.
PROVERBS 11:12

Tongue-chewing is still a worthwhile skill that I need to exercise even if it's painful.

Every grandparent has a treasure chest of great experience and information. We have fought the battles of parenthood. Some we won and some we definitely lost. Any young couple could benefit from what we've gone through. But that doesn't mean we should freely toss around advice.

When our children want advice on how to raise children, they need to ask. And if they ask, we should deliver our golden nuggets in very small handfuls. If someone yells for a life pre-server, he doesn't expect a truckload to be dumped on him.

I know why children argue at the dinner table. It would be easy to get them to stay in bed all night long. You don't need a gate on the stairway if you handle it right. I know exactly how to get them to eat their green vegetables without their throwing a fit. . . .

Certainly I know all of that and a lot more. All I have to do now is bite my tongue and keep my wisdom to myself. The best grandparents believe in holding their tongues.

ॐ

Lord, help me show respect for my children by not giving advice until asked.

A Wise Grandparent Knows...

THE ROLE OF A RESPONSIBLE MANAGER

⑤

Pat's Perspective

He must manage his own family well.

1 TIMOTHY 3:4

*O*ne Thursday morning when Bill was out of town, the grandchildren and I were at McDonald's for breakfast. While the children were having fun together in the playland, the manager's quiet demeanor and quick movements caught my eye.

He was neatly dressed and appeared to be in control of the environment. While overseeing the crew in the kitchen, most of whom spoke English as their second language, he was also checking that customers were being served quickly and courteously and that the dining area was clean and inviting. Quietly he was assisting a young male trainee.

It was obvious that the manager felt responsible for the property and people on and under his watch; he knew the answer or would find answers to every question. The restaurant ran like a well-oiled machine. As I admired his professional manner, it occurred to me that grandparents have a similar responsibility.

We are in charge of the safety and well-being of the children while they are with us. This responsibility calls for differing tactics, depending on a child's personality. Some children seem to be born with a fierce desire to do things for themselves. Others choose to let others do everything for them.

The ones who want to do for themselves seem to have no fear. They are the ones who get to know the doctor quite well. They are the ones with broken collarbones, scraped knees, and a few stitches. If a tree can be climbed, they will climb to the top. If something has wheels, they will see how fast it will go.

The ones who let you do everything for them seem to take forever learning to—or being motivated to—hang up or button up their own clothes or wash their hands. They require an extra dose of understanding in the early years.

Fortunately, most children are somewhere in the middle between the two extremes. Most have a sufficient amount of caution and inner drive to handle life well enough.

But the wise caretaker oversees their activities and sees that their needs are met. A responsible care-taking manager ponders the question: How much should I caution children of the dangers of being too adventuresome, and how much should I encourage the children to do it for themselves?

As managers we must handle any glitches in the day's activities. We step in to avoid dangers, and we wait while they put on their own coats. By our example, they are continuously learning to take care of themselves, to behave in a civil way, and to show respect to others.

Someday they will make decisions about their own well-being. Meanwhile we help them develop into responsible individuals.

§

Lord, give me wisdom to be a responsible manager when my grandchildren are in my care. May I know how to balance their need for encouragement and caution.

A Wise Grandparent Knows . . .

WHEN TO SAY NO

᭥

My son, pay attention to my wisdom,
listen well to my words of insight.

PROVERBS 5:1

*N*o!" said Grandmother.

Three-year-old Kelsey put her foot on the bottom rung and stood there. She and her grandmother locked eyes.

"You aren't going up the big slide. It's too dangerous."

Kelsey placed her second foot on the rung and looked down at the ground.

"One more step, and we go back to the car."

The stand-off lasted for five minutes. Grandmother had explained this before. It wasn't the way Grandmother wanted to interact.

We want to be warm-fuzzy fun all of the time, but sometimes we can't. There are lines that can't be crossed and battles that should not be lost.

Don't take it personally if a grandchild tests you to see what the boundaries are. Be prepared for tough days. This is the trying side of grandparenting.

Sometimes a parent—or a wise grandparent—simply has to say no. It's not too much to expect children to obey. "Children, obey your parents in the Lord" (Ephesians 6:1). If a parent is present, he or she is the best one to correct the child. If a parent is not present, it's up to grandparents.

Discipline is an essential part of life for both children and adults. When they are in your care, you must set boundaries for their safety and well-being and the well-being of everyone else. Generally correction isn't necessary because most grandchildren are eager to please a grandmother or grandfather.

When big brother is endangering baby, it's time to step in. When a child is stubbornly disobeying, it's time for an altercation. When the child is in a public place, proper behavior should be required.

Grandparents develop their individual methods of correcting a child. For some it is giving a time-out. For others it's sitting the child down and explaining that what they have done is unacceptable and will be punished. For some it's taking away privileges.

A gentle grandparent can correct firmly and effectively.

It's OK to have rules in your own home. If a grandparent wants the children to put away their toys or pick up clothes when they visit, he or she needs to state clearly and kindly the conduct that is expected and follow through. Some grandparents prefer a more relaxed environment; it's their choice.

Again, it's OK to have expectations when they are in your care. Your love for this child will help you figure out what will work for the two of you.

🌀

Lord, give me wisdom to know when to say no to these children I love—setting boundaries for their benefit, not because of my need for control.

THE TWO KINDS OF PRIDE

🌀

Parents are the pride of their children.
PROVERBS 17:6

One kind of pride is rightfully on the ancient list of seven deadly sins. Another kind seems healthy all around.

The first kind says, "I'm right. I'm the best. I know it all." As grandparents it's easy to fall into the trap; we huff and puff around as if this generation of young parents will never learn. Frankly, that act gets old real fast. Never let it be said of us what Job said of others: "You really know everything, don't you? And when you die, wisdom will die with you!" (Job 12:2 NLT).

Blessed are the parents whose parents know everything and keep most of it to themselves.

There is a great deal we didn't know about parenting when we raised kids. We still don't. Humble grandparents are all too rare. Wise grandparents have given up the job of raising children. They have moved on to the far better job of interacting with grandkids. The hours are better, the benefits more generous, you get more days off, and there is a terrific hug program.

Let us give you a glimpse of the second, good kind of pride. We saw it recently in the eyes and voice of our two-year-old grandson. When we were at our younger daughter's house, her son heard the back door open. That's all he heard. It wasn't a voice or a knock but only the sound of a door pushing away from the weather stripping. The toddler leaped to his feet and ran into the kitchen. "Daddy! Daddy!"

He hurried to his father's side, hugged his leg, turned, and they walked hand-in-hand into the living room. Standing side-by-side next to his dad, this young lad beamed with pride. "This is my dad" was written all over his smile.

We've seen this pride also in another set of grandchildren. Our older daughter occasionally puts on a puppet show at her church. The head puppet is a funny character named Ismeralda. Her orange hair is askew. Her dress has clashing colors and plaids, and she speaks in a screeching, domineering voice. The stage, made by a church-member carpenter, is a Victorian house with window panes, shutters, and shingles painted to perfection.

Standing side-by-side next to his dad, this young lad beamed with pride. "This is my dad" was written all over his smile.

When the puppet show begins, our grandchildren gather up front with the other children of the congregation. They aren't supposed to know that the puppet's voice is their mother's. But they know. Sitting there with wide grins and dancing eyes, they send out a message. They are enjoying this storytime immensely. And they are so proud of their mother.

And so are we.

ௌ

Lord, grant me the good kind of pride—that beams because I am pleased with and grateful for the children and grandchildren You have given me.

THE IMPORTANCE OF IMAGINATION

ⓢ

Bill's Perspective

"No eye has seen,
no ear has heard,
no mind has conceived
what God has prepared for those
who love him."

1 CORINTHIANS 2:9

nd on my last day there, the king of Brazil was so grateful that I had led the dinosaurs out of his country that he gave me a bucket of gold nuggets. The bucket was made of copper, and there were so many nuggets that they were stacked high above the rim."

Thus ended another of the Thursday lunchtime makebelieve stories I tell to my grandchildren about my inventions and adventures.

I leaned back into my chair, a round red apple in my hand. "Grandpa, what did you do with the bucket of gold nuggets?" the six-year-old asked. Her sparkling eyes told me she was trying her best to believe this tale.

"Right now I don't remember." I bit into the apple.

"Grandma," she persisted, "do you have the bucket of gold at your house?"

"Well," she stammered. "I've cleaned that house many times from attic to basement and never have seen a bucket of gold."

Our granddaughter looked into Grandma's eyes and pleaded, "Would you look one more time?"

We've spent many happy hours in the land of make-believe; there I remember inventing a wide array of items from cotton candy to straws, from bicycles to pizza, from chocolate to teaching. It's fun to get into trouble and out again, stretching everyone's imagination.

I have gotten into trouble more than once telling these stories. One granddaughter told her teacher there were still dinosaurs living on an island off Brazil. Grandpa said so. In another story I jumped on a bicycle when I was three and got away. My grandson reminded me that I didn't invent the bike until I was five. When I told them I invented teaching, they insisted that teaching was older than me, because there were teachers in the *Little House on the Prairie* books. Undaunted, I talked right through that one, too.

When you tell that many stories, you'd better hang loose.

There is a time to kid and tell fun stories; there is a time to relate true happenings; and there is a time to tell stories from the Bible. We try to be very clear so the children understand the difference.

Having said that, where better to take trips than running through the open fields of imagination? How can we exercise our robust faith in Jesus Christ if our imaginations are weak and stingy?

The Bible says: "Now to him who is able to do immeasurably more than all we ask or imagine, according to his power that is at work within us . . ." (Ephesians 3:20).

How often have we heard someone say, "I never thought to ask for that." Our imaginations are anemic. Our limited vision keeps us tied to the porch.

The imagination that remains stiff from lack of use can't begin to see what God might have for us.

"Did I ever tell you how I was shot into the air from a giant slingshot? Well, I remember it like it was yesterday. . . . "

๑

Lord, help me use my imagination to get a glimpse of how great You are.

A Wise Grandparent Knows . . .

THE VALUE OF BALANCE

There is a time for everything,
and a season for every activity under heaven.
ECCLESIASTES 3:1

"Sure, we'd love to come to the picnic," Linda assured them. "That is, unless we get a call, and 'they' want us to watch the grandchildren."

Barely fifty-five, Linda had put her life on hold, because she was always on call, ready to step in, any time or place, when and where she was needed to grandparent. She had moved into the regrettable category of what we call a professional grandparent. With possibly thirty more years to live, her interests had narrowed down to one priority. No one else mattered this much to her. Instead of remaining well-rounded with multiple interests and new adventures, she retreated to a single mission that could easily degenerate into an obsession.

"That's all she wants to do," complained her frustrated husband. "We used to go places, serve in organizations, even teach a Bible class. But now it's all wrapped into this." Grandparenting.

Our encouragement for you to be good and engaged grandparents is not a call to abandon the rest of life. At its best, grandparenting is part of a balanced relationship that still includes other opportunities, challenges, and even other fun.

Too many husbands and wives allow themselves to be pulled apart over this task. Let it be a *relationship* with grandchildren rather than a burdensome job.

85

The author of Ecclesiastes reminds us of the orderliness of life. Knowing there is an ebb and flow to life, wise people refuse to concentrate on one goal and one alone. They are not given to extremes. Granted, grandparents who have custodial care must function much as parents. However, even parents need other interests and take other roles, besides parenting.

The gifts and thoughtfulness of grandparents need to be measured out carefully. If we budget our time, much like a financial budget, we end up with more to distribute, not less.

Zig and zag, in and out, it involves knowing when to be available and when to attend to other things, when to say yes and when to say no. We are not professional grandparents.

§

Lord, give me wisdom to know when to be available and when to say no.

PART 5

For Grandchildren
A Caring Grandparent Models . . .

For Grandchildren a Caring Grandparent Models . . .

PATIENCE

⑤

Pat's Perspective

Clothe yourselves with . . . patience.
COLOSSIANS 3:12

It was county fair time.

One Thursday afternoon with three excited grandchildren in tow, we visited the 4-H exhibits, where we perused the photography, sewing, and mechanics projects and displays. Curiosity ran high. "Can we be 4-H'ers?" they asked.

Proud of their free 4-H stickers, they were off to the livestock barns: pens of rabbits, chickens, ducks, geese, cows, and even llamas. Their favorite was the horse barn and arena, where riders showed their stuff.

Finally we found the midway. We gave each child sixteen tickets, which meant about four rides. Alas, one of the girls bemoaned, "I wish it were like Worlds of Fun, where you can ride all day."

The limited number of tickets meant the kids had to make choices; they would not be able to ride everything. Nevertheless, they did a fine job of calculating how to use the tickets—for rides that required two, three, four, or five of them. With two tickets left over, one of the children wanted to sell them to his siblings. We stood back and watched the negotiations.

What a sight, especially when he had to lower his price to get a buyer.

When all the tickets were gone, we headed to the concession stand. Grandpa announced that everyone could choose a snack and a drink. His treat.

That's when Lesson 101 in grandparent patience came into play. The sign listed all the foods, but one of the children had seen someone licking a shaved ice drink, and it wasn't on the list. "I want one of those. Where can we get those?"

Ice cream was on the list, but another child needed to see all eight bars and Popsicles before choosing.

There were drinks in cups, drinks in cans, power drinks in bottles.

It took a long time for everyone to make up his or her mind. Bill and I were tired after trying to match the children's pace, which meant we had to draw deeply from our reservoir of patience until, finally, everyone was satisfied.

We were a happy bunch as we all sat together eating our treats.

In Galatians the apostle Paul names patience as a fruit of the Spirit, a characteristic that God imparts to us. But in Colossians Paul exhorts us to "clothe" ourselves with patience, as if we can make a conscious choice to put it on, like socks or shoes or a jacket. So it seems that there are two ways to come upon patience in a particular situation.

Six Tips for Being Patient with Children

1. As much as possible, give children 100 percent attention.
2. Slow down to their pace.
3. Listen well and hear what they say.
4. Speak and answer clearly, with gentleness.
5. Get a cup of coffee or take a break if you are getting uptight.
6. Remember, they are children.

Fortunately for me, my father was a sterling example. Putting on patience—it's a trait I want to model for my grandchildren.

ॐ

Lord, may my grandchildren find it easier to be patient because they see patience in me.

For Grandchildren a Caring Grandparent Models...

HUMILITY AND FLEXIBILITY

❧

Pat's Perspective

*Humble yourselves, therefore, under God's mighty
hand, that he may lift you up in due time. Cast all your
anxiety on him because he cares for you.*
1 PETER 5:6–7

It promised to be a fun day. My daughter and our two
granddaughters were coming over. Their dad, brother, and
Bill were out of town. The playroom was all ready. With beautiful weather, the girls could also play outside. *Great,* I thought.
I'll put on a pot of coffee, and we two ladies can sit and chat. The
opportunity to talk came so seldom anymore.

When they arrived, to my surprise Mom and the children
headed off together to the playroom. They had made plans on
the drive over to set up a play store.

So much for coffee and chatting.

I was a bit miffed as I headed to the kitchen to finish lunch.
For a few minutes I silently fumed as I sliced watermelon and
dropped corn-on-the-cob into the boiling water. These were
their favorite foods.

Soon I wised up and considered my options: Either I could
be irritated that it hadn't worked out as I hoped, or I could
jump in and have a fun day. I'm glad I chose the latter.

During our lunch we made plans together for the afternoon. We could go to the pool or to the library or to the play-

ground or make root beer floats or consider a host of other choices.

As the afternoon progressed, the girls put on a play, served a tea party, set up a museum, and went to the local Science Center. After supper we all voted to go to the park. There the children split off to play by themselves. Mom and I sat on the park bench and had a fabulous time catching up with each other's lives.

Being flexible that morning was paying huge dividends.

We adults—Bill and I and our children—rarely have the opportunity anymore to be together, go out to lunch, or take in a movie without children. Our interaction has moved to a different level. It takes humility to accept that we are no longer the most important people in the parents' lives. Fortunately the intergenerational friendship shifts and wiggles and encircles the changes that young children have brought.

Change is a given. Smart families find ways to keep friendships alive in new and different ways.

Instead of meeting for coffee, we now find other ways to fit into each other's lives:

- visiting around the dinner table after the children hop down to play;
- visiting after hours when the children are asleep;
- talking by phone, sending e-mail or letters.

Whatever works, grab it.

Roll with the punches and your children will call you blessed. And your grandchildren will notice your positive presence in their lives.

ᔕ

Lord, help me to be flexible, rather than demanding, in my expectations as I make plans.

GENTLENESS

🌀

Rejoice in the Lord always. I will say it again: Rejoice!
Let your gentleness be evident to all. The Lord is near.
PHILIPPIANS 4:4–5

A grown man stood in a store aisle looking down at a cute two-year-old girl. Her hair was pulled back in a neat ponytail. She wore red sneakers.

The white-haired man, almost three times her height and ten times her weight, towered over her and yelled at the top of his voice, "Why did you do that? Why did you do that? Has the cat stolen your ears? I don't know why I bother to take you anywhere."

Children live in a bewildering world of giants. The adults around are not only bigger, but also stronger, more experienced, louder, quicker, and often intimidating. The fortunate child meets a few gentle giants who bend down and are calm, patient, and forgiving. Grandparents could be those giants.

Grandparents don't need to say, "Go away; I'm busy." "Boy, you're a little pest." "Shame on you." "Can't you find something to do?" "Now don't ask me again."

Gentle giants have learned from experience. They aren't afraid to love or to listen or to look into the eyes of a puzzled child. Gentle giants have time to fix things. Paste things. Sew things. Clean things. Run things through the washer. They squat down—or sit if their knees are stiff—to be on the child's eye level.

They take out the backseat of the car and look for the lost blue button. They carry the two pennies home because a grandchild has no pockets. The same goes for leaves, sticks, stones, and half-eaten candy. They take time to show how the trunk of the car opens. They buy a box of four petunias, because they know a grandchild will love watching something grow.

Gentle giants pick up children and place them on their shoulders. They know they won't always be able to do this. But they know they had better do it while they can, standing beside a parade or walking hurriedly to catch up or simply giving rest to a child's tired legs. Grandparents know that gentleness is of great value. Water battles, wrestling matches, and loud laughter are valuable, but gentleness is too great a quality to miss. A value that must be passed on.

"Take my yoke upon you and learn from me, for I am gentle and humble in heart," Jesus said (Matthew 11:29). Jesus Christ was a gentle person. That should give me a clue of how important it is. I need never apologize for having a calm spirit if it was true of the Son of God.

Some grandparents get confused. They think they need to show harshness because we live in a harsh and nasty world. The truth is, we had better demonstrate gentleness because we live in a harsh and nasty world.

Let every child know and remember that he once knew a gentle person. He will love that gentle person forever.

⑤

Lord, may gentleness be part of my voice and actions. May it ease the harshness that children face from time to time.

LOVE FOR SCRIPTURE
AND PRAYER

🌀

From infancy you have known the holy Scriptures, which are able to make you wise for salvation through faith in Christ Jesus.

2 TIMOTHY 3:15

In this Scripture verse, Paul is reminding Timothy of the Scriptures that he learned at the knee of his grandmother, Lois.

Picture little Timothy sitting on a stool or perched on the floor at mealtime. His grandmother, Lois, kneels by his side. They both clench their hands and squeeze their eyes closed. They pray before or after they eat to thank a loving God for the food He continues to provide.

One of our greatest satisfactions is watching our two-year-old grandson sitting in a high chair waiting to eat. He clenches his chubby hands together, squints his eyes tightly shut, and gets ready to pray.

Reading Bible stories at the breakfast table—that's what grabs one granddaughter's attention. She loves scrambled eggs, toast, sausage, fruit, and Jonah and Moses. Pulling out a children's Bible storybook, she loves to choose the stories she wants to hear—sometimes six at a time; the more action the better. She salts her eggs while the walls of Jericho come crashing down. Elijah and the prophets of Baal shout out prayers while she eats sausage links. Our granddaughter loves the colorful pictures. She enjoys the short story format. That's her idea of a good time: toast, Jonah, and a whale in the morning. All traditions have to start somewhere. This one began at a breakfast table one Thursday morning.

That's her idea of a good time: toast, Jonah, and a whale in the morning.

Many Christians say how tired they are of the old routines they went through at home. They have resolved not to repeat those with their grandchildren. But instead of throwing routine away, why not look for new and different ways to share, even in less formal and predictable ways.

Any one of us can be as influential to the spiritual lives of our grandchildren as Lois was to Timothy, a young man whose good reputation we still respect, two thousand years after he lived.

§

Lord, may our love for Your Word come across to our grandchildren. And may they see that we depend on You in prayer and as we read Your Word.

For Grandchildren a Caring Grandparent Models...

COURAGE

✺

Bill's Perspective

"Be strong and courageous. Do not be terrified; do not be discouraged, for the LORD your God will be with you wherever you go."

JOSHUA 1:9

hy not? He was only four years old, but he might really enjoy it. I decided to take my grandson on a tour of the local soft drink plant. We could see how a modern operation works and maybe get a free sample.

When I first talked about this, some wise person immediately asked me if the soft drink plant conducted tours.

That seemed like a silly and negative question. Certainly any self-respecting soft drink plant would hold tours for children.

"Why don't you give them a call and find out?" suggested another nay-sayer. Telephones just get in the way, I reasoned.

The only civilized way to find out is to drive down and take the tour. We will not be discouraged easily. On the basis of that logic I enthusiastically informed my young companion of our Thursday goal.

When we arrived, I did notice that there wasn't a busload of tourists. But I marched in anyway.

"Good morning. We would like to take a tour of your plant," I explained to the receptionist.

Pause. "I don't think we offer a tour," she replied, a bit flustered. "Wow," I countered. "My grandson has really been looking forward to this."

She reluctantly picked up the phone. "I'll check."

"Mr. Bateman," she said, "there is a gentleman here with his four-year-old grandson. They want to take a tour of the plant."

Another pause.

"I said," she repeated, "there is a gentleman down here with his four-year-old grandson. They want to tour. . . . "

A longer pause.

She hung up.

"Mr. Bateman, our vice-president, will be right down." She smiled. I was encouraged.

That's how it came to be: our first-class inspection of the premises. We were both impressed with the vice-president's knowledge of the facilities as well as his personal charm. And yes, when he bade us a fine farewell, he was kind enough to serve us a round of cold drinks.

There is no way I would have gone to the plant alone. Normally I'm not that bold when I'm by myself and acting on behalf of my own interests. But with a grandchild by my side, the two of us together can rise up to take on all sorts of challenges. Courage, without crassness, is a terrific trait, one that God wants us all to exhibit in our daily lives. It's a virtue I'm honing because of—and with the help of—my grandchildren. With them—and God—at my side, who knows what we'll explore next?

ᑐ

Lord, give me courage without crassness because of and with the help of my grandchildren.

For Grandchildren a Caring Grandparent Models . . .

PEACEMAKING

🌀

But the wisdom that comes from heaven is first of all pure; then peace-loving.

JAMES 3:17

The divorce was nasty and several things were said that should have been kept quiet. In one exchange "his" parents got overheated and added their two cents. Now "she" would no longer answer phone calls from her ex-in-laws.

Before long the grandparents received a letter saying they would no longer be permitted to see the two children. If the grandparents continued to contact her, she threatened to move out of the state and not tell them where.

Their relationship had never been particularly close, but the grandparents didn't foresee this. They certainly hadn't done everything right, but now their hearts were broken. Tuesday afternoon was their appointment with a lawyer to see what action they needed to take.

Stories like this are being told in offices and courtrooms all across the country. A son dies and the parents want the motorcycle back that they had bought for him before the marriage. A mother remarries and takes the children into a religious commune. In situation after troubling situation, grandparents are fighting to have access to their grandchildren.

There are no quick or easy solutions, but there may be a good place to start. We need to ask what is most important, and we need to aim for peace. Would we fight over the ownership of a car and lose the grandchildren? Would we break relationships over how the child is baptized? Would we give up a grandchild by arguing over where his birthday party will be?

In the Sermon on the Mount Jesus taught,

"Blessed are the peacemakers,
for they will be called sons of God."
                                        MATTHEW 5:9

Grandparents, whenever possible, must keep peace with children and in-laws. They do the work of God when they refuse to fight over things that are of no lasting value.

None of us dares judge another grandparent. Who are we to say how we might act or what action we might take under certain circumstances? We can only imagine the pain that would come from being denied our grandchildren.

One of the few things we do know is that a primary goal is to seek peace. That is a priceless gift we can give to our grandchildren, ourselves, and everyone involved.

God seems to be more pleased by peace than by perfectly correct heirloom distribution.

ⓖ

Lord, may I draw on Your unending supply of wisdom
and wherever possible be a blessed peacemaker.

For Grandchildren a Caring Grandparent Models...

APPRECIATION

❦

Pat's Perspective

I commend to you our sister Phoebe. . . .
ROMANS 16:1

*I*f grandparents aren't careful, they forget to praise today's parents. Often today's parents are modern-day heroes. Faced with difficult choices, they sacrifice and struggle and love deeply to raise their children.

When a grandchild has just told Bill something fun he or she did with a parent, I often hear Bill respond: "Boy, you sure have a nice mom and dad." A truckload of compliments, praise, and recognition is due these responsible adults. They provide for the children, keep close tabs on their health and safety, get them to bed on time, teach basic human decency, and so much more—all with a patient and loving attitude. Consider the following true scenario:

All three children were sick with the flu. Mommy made beds for them on couches in the living room and brought books, games, and toys. With fevers raging, stomachs upset, bodies becoming dehydrated, they were pitiful little figures. Finally, on the fourth day, after tending them day and night, Mommy, now on overload, also succumbed to the virus.

I phoned and offered to come and help.

"Thank you, but we're doing OK. We really don't want you coming in and being exposed to this." Daddy was staying home to care for his family.

My admiration for that family rose another notch. Their sense of values demanded they not spread the virus to outsiders, and their sense of responsibility required they take care of their own family.

Over a recent cup of coffee, a friend who is also a grandmother and I talked about how good life is at our age. We can come and go as we like, pursue our interests, and take trips with our husbands from time to time. Then our conversation moved to what life is like for our grown children. "I don't know how they do it," one of us said. Caring for little children, keeping house and home together, feeding and clothing their families, tending to broken collarbones and broken hearts, juggling time for church and school activities—it all seems overwhelming. An evening out is a rare treat for them.

Yesterday our daughter phoned to thank me for the lodging and food at our house over Thanksgiving. She said what an enjoyable time her family had. My reply? "Thank you for coming. Hosting a holiday get-together doesn't begin to compare with what you two do every day as parents. We think you are great."

A sincere word of commendation does wonders for a parent's sagging spirit.

Our grandchildren are blessed indeed to have noble and trustworthy parents such as these.

⅁

Lord, help me gift my children with affirmation. May I speak words of encouragement and acknowledge their tenacity in parenting so well.

PART 6

❀

Special Words for Special Grandparents

CUSTODIAL GRANDPARENTS

❦

The LORD disciplines those he loves,
as a father the son he delights in.

PROVERBS 3:12

At age forty-six, Beth wasn't looking for a six-year-old and a two-year-old to raise, but one day she agreed to take on that responsibility—taking in her grandchildren. Her daughter's life was in disarray. Considering her problems, the young woman seemed to be choosing the right path, deciding to drop out of the parental role.

Frankly, Beth was a little more enthused about the project than her husband. But to his credit he mustered up a good spirit. Soon he was taking the children out for milkshakes and reading books about fuzzy creatures. Sometimes he complained about missing time with Beth, but usually he jumped in with both feet.

Early on, Beth and her husband had to make some serious decisions. Both of them wanted to be grandparents; they wanted to indulge the children, take them places on school nights, and buy them candy. But quickly they ran into reality. There was no way they could be both parents and grandparents. They would have to choose.

Usually the difference is clear. Parents stereotypically say things like, "No, it's your bedtime. Pick up your toys. You have two minutes to get in there and brush your teeth. You don't get to watch any television tonight."

Grandparents may take another tack: "It's only ten o'clock. Let's play another game. Would you like to eat some ice cream while we play? Wait right here, and I'll get it for you. I think I have some of those special cookies you like so well."

Beth and her husband wanted to be indulgent grandparents, but they knew that wasn't going to work at this stage. They would have to put "grandparenting" on hold and reclaim that role when they became great-grandparents. They still had time.

Custodial grandparents who act like regular grandparents can expect big problems. Children need parents, of any age, who follow through with parental duties. For any number of reasons, including death, incarceration, or drug or alcohol abuse, sometimes adult children vacate the scene and leave their young children in a lurch. Fortunately, some of these children have grandparents who will step up to the bat when needed.

Custodial grandparents usually make excellent parents. They have experience and wisdom. They aren't like most parents who learn on the job and finally understand it all when it's too late. Grandparents have had the training and see ways to do it differently the second time around.

Sadly, a few custodial grandparents get confused about the job at hand. Custodial grandparenting calls for energy, discipline, dedication, and creativity, as well as that old favorite, stubbornness. Freshly baked cookies, trips to theme parks, and new teddy bears, while nice, will never substitute for good parenting skills.

Maybe there's a good reason why Jesus taught us to pray to "our Father" in heaven and not "our Grandfather." The way I see it, parents, including grandparents who parent, do the work of God. They guide and discipline children who sorely need their direction.

Lord, give Your special direction to those grandparents who are guardians for their grandchildren.

SINGLE GRANDPARENTS

🌀

*If a widow has children or grandchildren, these should
learn first of all to put their religion into practice by caring for their own family and so repaying their parents
and grandparents, for this is pleasing to God.*

1 TIMOTHY 5:4

The white-haired woman spoke excitedly about her life.
Her good husband had been dead for a decade or more.
He had provided reasonably well for her, and she had considerable free time. What was she doing to fill up her life? Just
"killing time" wasn't an option for her.

Every Friday, she explained, she got into her car and drove
150 miles to see her grandchildren. Her wonderful daughter
and son-in-law had fixed up a room for her. Friday nights
through Sunday afternoons, she played and planned with the
grandchildren. The parents could go on a date, fix the plumb-
ing, or get ready for church on Sunday. Grandma often cooked
a meal or two, helped shine shoes, or pitched softball. On
Sunday afternoons she latched her seatbelt, waved good-bye,
and headed home until next Friday. Grandma also had responsibilities at home.

Widows or widowers aren't the only single grandparents
out there. Millions of divorced grandparents are taking similar roles, helping out as they are able and willing.

After a meeting, a woman came over and shared this story
with us. Like the woman mentioned above, she began to make

weekly trips to see the grandkids. After they ironed out a few wrinkles, everyone got along great, despite the fact that they had no guest bedroom. Finally her son declared his solution to this inconvenience. They had a big yard; he wanted to build her a house right out back. That was the way they had done it in the old days, he pointed out. (You might call it a grandmother apartment.) Before long he was drawing up plans and digging footings.

Many grandparents who live alone have grandchildren who would love to hear from them.

The world is crowded with lonely people. Either by choice or necessity, many of us have become increasingly isolated, torn apart rather than drawn together. It is not too late to reverse that trend. Many grandparents who live alone have grandchildren who would love to hear from them. They cherish time together with grandparents who make them feel special.

Any of us can turn our isolation to prayer, even as we look for ways to better connect with our children and grandchildren. If we let our minds be wide open to anything from the practical to the ridiculous, maybe we can think of ways to get to know our grandchildren better.

Grandchildren are terrific bridge builders. Often they are the key to finding renewed love with our own children.

⑤

Lord, I know it doesn't take two grandparents to connect with grandchildren. Show me ways to be useful without interfering.

GRANDCHILDREN OF A DIFFERENT CULTURE

🌀

And a little child will lead them.
ISAIAH 11:6

$\mathcal{G}$ary was not an easy person to be around. He tended to
be rude, crude, and loud. Never was he more difficult
than when he was making racial slurs. Native Americans,
African Americans, Asians, Latinos, all were referred to in vul-
gar slang. No one seemed to know where he developed such
a nasty attitude, but he certainly wore it on his sleeve.

All of that was true until one day when he walked into the
coffee shop with a wide grin on his face. Gary sat down and
proudly announced that his daughter in Seattle had just
adopted a beautiful Asian child. In his muscle-bound, weather-
worn hand he held the photo of his tiny grandchild.

Don't think that this totally changed crusty Gary. He still
leaned toward intolerance and distrust, but what a difference,
nevertheless. He melted around the edges. Never again was he
as quick to condemn or as sweeping in his prejudices.

This wasn't the first time, and it won't be the last, when a
little child has led an adult to a higher plane. When loud voices
and threats fail to make an impact, an infant often has a way
of reaching into our hearts and turning the knobs. And sometimes that influential child is a grandchild.

One fall evening a sixty-year-old mother received a knock
on her door. She welcomed her nervous daughter into her

apartment, and they sat down. The daughter got straight to the subject. She and her husband had an excellent opportunity to adopt a child from Mexico. They were about to go ahead, she explained, but they felt they should take time to check with their parents first. How would she feel about being the grandmother to a Mexican grandchild?

With tears in her eyes, the older woman wrapped her arms around her daughter. "How soon can I meet my grandchild?" was all she wanted to know.

We no longer live in small, closed, even controlled, communities. More Americans are marrying and adopting outside of their racial or ethnic backgrounds. Frequently we will see our grandchildren raised in churches or houses of worship that we would not have selected. But millions of grandparents are welcoming diversity into their homes with open arms.

Some things we have trouble accepting until we have children of our own. Only then do we realize how narrow-minded we were. Other changes are so hard and we are so stubborn that we need grandchildren to come along and deliver us.

If it takes a little child . . . we pray you will open your heart. Take a leap. Let love slip out. Let love rush in.

ᕼ

Lord, thank You for making me a better person because of what I learn from little children.

SURROGATE GRANDPARENTS

Bill's Perspective

"'Love the Lord your God with all your heart and with all your soul and with all your strength and with all your mind'; and, 'Love your neighbor as yourself.'"
LUKE 10:27

Saturday was a great day to go to a ballgame. Bryan had three tickets to see the Trojans play football, and he was taking Kevin and Aaron along. The grade-school kids were brothers who lived two doors down. Bryan's children were grown, so he looked for ways to get together with these neighbor boys.

Bryan thoroughly enjoyed the role of substitute grandparenting. The boys' mother had all she could handle with a full-time job, so he liked to help out. Bryan had some extra time plus lots of toys left over from his parenting days. Once in a while his wife fixed a special meal for the children and invited them over for the evening.

By simple acts like this, several needs were being met. Bryan and his wife considered it a way to serve and minister to others. The young mother received some relief; and of course the boys loved the attention.

Not all of us have grandchildren nearby. So why not look around and find some? Our grandchildren might live a thousand miles away, but we can still take a couple of wide-eyed children to the local circus.

One Sunday in church I watched a two-year-old run down the aisle and leap into the arms of a man with graying hair. The older brother and sister soon followed and wrapped their arms around the man's wife. These were surrogate grandchildren. Once a week the man and his wife invited the kids over to cook, play, and learn to love one another.

However long these relationships might last, the feelings of acceptance and caring can last forever. Someone reached out in a nonjudgmental way and gathered in a child in need of love and attention: That act of love will travel with that child the rest of his or her life.

Jesus told us to love our neighbors. A person in need becomes our neighbor, whether that person lives next door or across town or further away. Whether that person is a child of five or ten or fifteen.

When Pat's grandmother died, a loving aunt stepped in to give Pat's two-year-old sister extra attention and love. The aunt invited little sister over for weekend visits, took her on special outings, and seemed always to sense how much the little girl needed a grandmother-like touch. She made the little girl feel special.

As Pat's little sister grew, this dear aunt remained a stable tent peg for the girl. If you've ever pitched a tent, you know how necessary strong tent pegs are. The aunt was doing the work of God.

ᘐ

Lord, if there is a child who needs my attention as a surrogate parent, show me the role you want me to have in this young life.

DIVORCE AND GRANDPARENTS

🌀

The LORD is close to the brokenhearted
and saves those who are crushed in spirit.

PSALM 34:18

Standing by the church doors, tossing rice, no one ever thought these two would divorce, but they did. Holiday meals, prayers, visits, and babysitting weren't enough to glue them together.

Now it's over, and everyone got hurt. Parents screamed, children worried, and all the grandparents grieved. No matter how or why, nothing stopped the train wreck, and now Mom and Dad have gone their separate ways.

Children of divorced parents often leave grandparents at a loss for words. What can they say? They try not to take sides, but they do have feelings, and some of their strongest feelings might even point toward their own children.

What are grandparents going to do? How can they reach out and help the grandchildren they love? It takes more than a simple list, but here are a few do's. And the sidebar gives a few don'ts.

1. Keep your word. It's more important than ever that your grandchild trust you. If you say you will be there Wednesday, be there Wednesday. If you said eight o'clock, don't arrive at nine.
2. Assure the children of your love and acceptance. This can diminish any suspicions that the divorce was somehow

their fault or that there was or is something wrong with them.

3.   Reassure them of God's love. There is no telling what the child might think. Is divorce a way of punishing the child? Is God angry at the entire family? Does God's love remain steady as a rock? Tell children God loves everyone involved. It's good to know that God isn't picking sides.

4.   Read to the child. Few practices are as healthy, comforting, and strengthening as the calming voice of a caring grandparent reading to a child. The message is clear: There are some people you can count on.

5.   Invite the children over. The playroom and the kitchen with the warm aroma of baking cookies are welcoming and calming. Be fun.

6.   Listen, listen, listen. When your grandchildren want to talk, be totally available. They need someone to bounce ideas off of. We may not know the answers, but at least we hear the questions. Good listeners are better than good answers.

A Few Divorce-Don'ts for Grandparents

1.   Don't put either parent down. Grandchildren have enough trouble adjusting without another person taking potshots at one of the parents.

2.   Don't defend either parent. If a parent isn't keeping his promises, don't protect that parent. Simply say, "Why don't you ask him or her why he or she did that?"

3.   Don't interrogate the children. They may begin to distrust you and stop talking.

4.   Don't feel sorry for the child. It only makes the child feel worse. Divorce is hard enough without piling on sympathy. Keep a balance and move the child from strength to strength.

All of us need purpose in our lives. If the pain of divorce hits our grandchild, God may want us to rise up to do some of His work. Psalm 34:18 notes that His work is to mend a broken spirit.

Grandparents are made for times like this.

⑤

Lord, may we be sensitive to those who hurt.

Special Words for Special Grandparents
GRANDPARENTS AT A DISTANCE

⑤

Even in laughter the heart may ache.
PROVERBS 14:13

gotta be honest with you," a young dad said haltingly. "It's just too far. I only get two weeks of vacation every year, and we can't spend all of it driving out here to see you guys.

"Soon the kids will be involved in even more activities. They want to go to camp and theme parks with their friends. We aren't going to be able to set aside two weeks every year for our visit."

No one wanted to say it and no one wanted to hear it, but the truth was obvious. Grandparenting from a considerable distance can be a heartbreaker. The solution for some has been to move closer; for others it is neither practical nor preferable. For instance, what does a grandparent do if there are four children living in four separate states?

Living far apart will never be like living down the street. However, there are several ways to maximize the possibilities.

First, keep the communication up. Technology has greatly expanded our options. There's old-fashioned letter-writing, photos, and mailed presents, supplemented by audiotapes, telephones, videos, e-mail. When these are used with a loving touch, grandchildren may be eager to get into the action and reciprocate.

One daughter writes a newsy letter each week telling of the activities and interests of her child. "Getting that letter is the highlight of our week," said the grandmother. When they visit, the grandparents have plenty to talk about, because they know what has been going on in their granddaughter's life.

Second, plan short and/or dual-purpose visits. What other sights—side trips—might the family enjoy on the way to grandmother's house? One hopes grandparents can also visit on a regular basis. Just don't stay too long.

Third, encourage a surrogate grandparent. Maybe there is someone in the grandchildren's church, neighborhood, or social group who enjoys being with the children. Don't be jealous or negative.

Distance doesn't always have to be measured in sadness.

Turn the green light on. Tell a child how happy you are that she found someone; you can hardly wait to meet the person when you come to visit.

Distance doesn't always have to be measured in sadness. Anyone who spends the time to reach out across the miles can find great happiness in getting to know the child who seldom gets to stand in line in front of him at McDonald's. Keep the creative juices flowing. Mail a cheerful picture, a zany video, music tapes, a short book accompanied by a tape of the grandparent reading it, a bedtime message every night for a week at a time, a little spending money. . . . Send a happy hug into a grandchild's life.

None of that will take the ache away. But it can add joy to a sense of disappointment.

🌀

Lord, show us how to stay in touch with our grandchildren who live at a distance.

PART 7

๑

A Good Grandparent Gives . . .

A Good Grandparent Gives . . .

THE GOLDEN GIFT OF READING

"Do you understand what you are reading?" Philip asked.

"How can I," he said, "unless someone explains it to me?" So he invited Philip to come up and sit with him. . . .

Then Philip began with that very passage of Scripture and told him the good news about Jesus.

ACTS 8:30–31, 35

He worked for Candace, the queen of Ethiopia. Because his job was so important, he often got to travel in the royal chariot. To pass the time, he sometimes read whatever book was available. Back then one always read aloud, and one day someone gave him a book written by a man named Isaiah.

To his surprise a man named Philip ran up to the chariot and asked, "Do you understand what you are reading?"

"Not a clue," he answered, or words to that effect. "Why don't you climb up here and explain it to me? Tell me, who is the person Isaiah has written about in this book?"

Then Philip explained that the author was telling the reader about Jesus.

We can hardly exaggerate the importance of reading. It is a golden gift with three leaves, like a shamrock: reading silently or aloud, being read to, and having someone answer questions when we don't understand.

When one grandmother prepares for her grandchildren's visit, she hurries off to the library. She adds to her personal col-

OUR FAMILY'S FAVORITES

Our grandchildren like almost any colorful book with pictures. One that has been especially popular is the pop-up book *All Things Bright and Beautiful* published by Tyndale House. Another favorite is an oversized nursery rhyme book that was Pat's as a child. As they have gotten older, they love chapter books, such as *The Boxcar Children.*

lection by taking out twenty-five or thirty volumes for the weekend. Where she lives, the libraries are particularly generous to grandparents. Returning home, she spreads the books around the house. Setting out a thick blanket and some pillows, she arranges a "reading area" in the corner of the living room.

Knowing that won't be nearly enough books for a weekend, early Saturday morning Grandma and two grandchildren head off to the library. "Are we almost there?" the children keep asking, as they walk the five blocks.

At the library they scurry to the reading pit (which the children call the rest pit). For an hour they read, are read to, and ask Grandma to explain words to them. When finished, they start the long trek back to Grandma's house, still asking, "Are we almost there yet?"

The weekend is jammed full of swinging, sandboxes, wrestling, park safaris, swimming, board games, computer games. . . . But in between activities, they all drift back to read another book or two. Or maybe a favorite, making that age-old plea: "Grandma, read it again."

ॐ

Lord, as I introduce these children to good books, help them learn to love to read.

A Good Grandparent Gives . . .

ONE-ON-ONE ATTENTION

§

Pat's Perspective

And the two of them went on together.
GENESIS 22:8

When our youngest grandchild was five months old, his parents, brother, their cousins, and their parents decided it was time for a weekend vacation at Worlds of Fun.

We were the lucky ones chosen to keep the baby.

For days ahead I had thought of just where to put his crib, what toys to bring out, and what we might do together. It was our chance to get to know each other very well.

It had been a long time since I had cared for such a little one; would I remember how?

He was a good teacher. I soon found out that he loved being held. That was easy to do. I also learned that he liked our morning walks around the neighborhood. When a little one is content and smiling, you know he's happy.

But one of his favorite things was taking a bath. His little body would wiggle with delight when he saw the tub. Lying on the spongy cushion, he excitedly kicked his chubby legs and waved his arms. His smiles showed total enjoyment.

I also learned that he preferred to have his shoulders and head elevated when lying on the floor. That way he could see what was going on. A pillow propped him up just fine.

Being a good eater, he always let me know if I had the temperature just right for the milk in his bottle. He communicated well.

Bill and I learned early that it's fun to have several children visit together, but the very best time is when they visit one-on-one. At first we wondered if they'd be lonesome without a sibling, but they seem to have the most fun when on their solo trips.

They feel special. Doing things together is without interruption. At home they always have siblings sharing the attention of the parents, but when they come alone to Grandpa's, they are the focus of activities.

Sitting at our table and laughing together, on a couch reading books, going to the park, in each case, a grandchild will be listened to; his or her choices can be honored. We can go at the child's pace—because it's just one child. Grandma will fix favorite foods. Grandpa will take the child on outings.

Not just when a grandchild visits us, but also when we are at our grandchildren's houses, one-on-one is great. My granddaughter and I won't soon forget strapping on her roller skates, helmet, elbow, knee and ankle protectors and heading down the sidewalk to the nearest snack bar. Side by side we go at her pace, close together so she has someone to grab if she starts to fall. When we arrive at our destination, we take off the gear and go in for ice cream bars. At the table, conversation rolls, and we learn more about each other. You can't beat one-on-one for getting to know a friend and building a relationship.

🌀

Lord, thank You for golden hours together with my friend.

A Good Grandparent Gives . . .

THE SOUND OF MUSIC

🌀

Bill's Perspective

Let the heavens rejoice, let the earth be glad;
*   let the sea resound, and all that is in it;*
*   let the fields be jubilant, and everything in them.*
Then all the trees of the forest will sing for joy.

PSALM 96:11–12

"J want music! I want music, please!"

With a winning smile, our two-year-old grandson has a gift for telling you what he wants. He even makes the effort to say *please*.

I stop the car by the side of the road, get out, and search around in the toy box in the backseat. Securing the cassette, I return to the driver's seat and punch in the tape.

Tooling down the highway, we soon have a songfest. Grandson, grandfather, and tape all sing a similar note and imagine that we are exactly on key.

We manage to produce a fine rendition of "Jesus Loves Me" with genuine gusto and joy. It's good to be reassured that the Bible tells us so—as merrily we roll along. The alphabet song runs us through our paces. Then there is the school bus song. The wheels go round and round, the babies go wa-wa-wa, and naturally the mothers say shh-shh-shh.

A grandparent's singing should be above criticism, but recently a couple of grandchildren have requested that I not sing along. That didn't hurt my feelings, but I did take note.

Their parents are responsible for most of the classical or more polished music in their lives. We've learned to use this to good advantage; we discovered that if we put stringed Christian music on the CD player, a roomful of grandchildren will calm down to a whisper. They turn to reading, playing board games, even falling into naps on the floor. Subtly symphony transforms cacophony.

So one day as if by inspiration, it dawned on me how boring car rides must be for kids these days. A child typically sits strapped into the backseat for thirty minutes until we arrive at our destination. If we try to talk, even in a loud voice, we both miss a third of what the other says.

That's when I saw the light. We needed tapes. Music tapes to feed our brains above the road noise. Singing tapes to lift our spirits as we rolled along.

The psalmist told us that nature is alive with music. Certainly our grandchildren could heartily join into that choir of joy, wonder, and praise. Singing adds a great dimension of spiritual life for both those who listen and those who participate. Even if occasionally we are asked not to sing—please.

ᔆ

Lord, at home or in the car, remind me to give my grandchildren the gift of music.

A CHRISTIAN HERITAGE

☙

Pat's Perspective

For you have heard my vows, O God;
*   you have given me the heritage of those who fear*
*   your name.*

PSALM 61:5

All he had to say was, "Sorry. There's no room at the inn."
It wasn't a big part, but no one doubted its importance. How could you have a Christmas play without an
innkeeper to deliver the news?

No matter, our grandson was having none of it. And he
wasn't about to wear that funny head covering. His younger
siblings have participated every year, dressing up as angels,
dutifully prancing around, singing delightful songs, and saying lines on cue. But year after year, he didn't want to participate. He didn't like being a shepherd. He didn't enjoy singing.
Even standing alone as a guard and saying nothing was more
of an investment than he wanted to make.

One year he played Joseph (a nonspeaking part). Suddenly
in the middle of the pageant, he had to go to the restroom.
Wisely, he left the stage immediately. The actors paused,
patiently waiting for Mary's husband to return. When the
unplanned intermission seemed awkwardly long, the narrator
announced calmly, "Joseph is out watering the donkeys."

Frankly, a future in acting appeared hopeless. The best he could do was stand in a corner, as a tree. Hopeless, that is, until his parents received a picture in the mail. That photo gave them a glimpse of the possibilities. The photo was of a church play, a Christmas play, no less. All of the actors and actresses were dressed in costumes and had bright smiles and beaming eyes. And there in the corner, dressed as an angel, sitting in a rocking chair, was our grandson's great-grandmother—my ninety-two-year-old mother.

If we had advice to give, it would be this: Our grandson might just as well get with the program. With a strong heritage like this, he doesn't have a chance. He may as well get used to wearing bathrobes and singing "Joy to the World." He may have eighty years of Christmas programs to look forward to.

A godly heritage can give our children and grandchildren a sense of where they've been; it helps young people decide where they want to go.

Often those who have difficulties in life have not been given a sense of values. They are uneasy with their past and have trouble dealing with the future.

A godly Christian isn't everything, but it's something. May our grandson always be able to picture his great-grandmother, in angel garb, in the nativity scene. May this, maybe her last gift to him, help him choose to take his place in the body of Christ—whether or not he ever ends up on stage.

ॐ

Lord, thank You for those in our families who loved and honored You.

A Good Grandparent Gives...

SEEDS OF FAITH

❧

Bill's Perspective

"It is like a mustard seed, which is the smallest seed you plant in the ground. Yet when planted, it grows and becomes the largest of all garden plants, with such big branches that the birds of the air can perch in its shade."

MARK 4:31–32

Grandmother Daisy was of another generation. Her home still had a potbellied woodstove, and the house sat alongside a country road. Most summer days she wore a bonnet and enjoyed picking beans or other vegetables from her large garden.

I, her thirteen-year-old grandson, hardly knew what to expect when I arrived at her door one summer day, satchel in hand. I was there to spend ten days with an elderly woman I hardly knew.

The only previous visit I remembered was for my grandfather's funeral. Grandfather's body had been laid out in a coffin in the parlor, and I, frightened, had not slept at all that night. The upstairs bedroom wasn't far enough away to offer any comfort or peace.

During the new visit, I roamed around the countryside every day. A city dweller had a great deal to investigate in the country. There were trees to climb, streams to follow, and a goat by the small pond. After devoting an hour or more to trying to give the goat a bath, I smelled so foul I was no longer fit to enter the house.

That visit, thirty miles north of Baltimore, leaves a dozen good memories, but none more impressive than this: Grandmother, who seldom spoke, sat quietly beside the window both morning and evening and read her Bible.

There was little evidence of faith in the home where I grew up. I'm not sure what my parents believed; they never talked about it. But what I saw at Grandmother's was most profound. I didn't know people read so intently, so religiously. It was one of the first times a living faith ever registered with me.

Small acts of faith are often carried on from generation to generation.

Two years later I invited Christ into my life.

Small acts of faith are often carried on from generation to generation, even if one generation's beliefs grow dim while the next generation's shine brighter. What helps carry faith on? It's often little acts that leave a lasting impression.

When Jesus saw a widow put two coins in the offering, He praised her for giving the little that she had. With no wealth to offer up, she shared what she could. " 'I tell you the truth,' he said, 'this poor widow has put in more than all the others'" (Luke 21:3). Good grandparents share their faith however they can. Some preach sermons; others read books. Many pray and sing. Still others show a great example. We don't all do it the same. But whatever we share registers with children and echoes throughout their lives.

Grandparents who plant even "mustard seeds" of faith may see that faith become vibrant and strong as their grandchildren grow.

၆

Lord, help me, by word and deed, to plant seeds of faith in the lives of my grandchildren.

A Good Grandparent Gives...

INDIVIDUALIZED ENCOURAGEMENT

§

Pat's Perspective

Train up a child in the way he should go and in keeping with his individual gift or bent, and when he is old he will not depart from it.

PROVERBS 22:6 AMPLIFIED

*D*o you know the scenario—perceiving adorable or admirable traits in your grandchildren when you previously would have rolled your eyes at those same silly traits in other children?

My six-year-old granddaughter and I walked to the grocery store to get bananas. Just as we were about to enter the automatic door, she darted off to the newspaper machines to check the coin slots for loose change.

How resourceful, I thought. Then we proceeded into the store to the produce aisle where we chose some fresh fruit. As we were about to enter the checkout, she noticed pop machines and scooted over to scout those coin slots. Patiently I waited, amused at what a clever little girl she was.

Good grandparents notice the unique characteristics and interests of each child and try to build on those traits in ways that encourage each individual.

Our two-year-old grandson loves to be outside. From the time he awakens in the morning until time to go to bed at night, he is happy to be in the backyard, walking around town, playing at parks, and going places. That suits me to a T.

On the other hand, another grandchild's favorite thing is having pens, paper, magic markers, a computer, or anything at hand with which she can create books and cartoons. I admire her skills and expertise and try to be a cheerleader and participant in her projects.

Then another grandchild loves to play alone. She has a special lighted closet at our big old house where she plays house. I save unusual-shaped boxes, trivets, wall hangings, and outdated kitchen items for her room.

The baby loves to go for walks, but he prefers not to go in a stroller. Bundling him up in a soft blanket, I took him in my arms and went for a walk on a recent evening. The street was quiet. The streetlights had just come on. The moon and stars were peeking out. As I cradled his behind in the crook of my arm, he stretched his neck to see what was ahead of us, down the sidewalk. So he could see better, I turned him to face forward. He peered at the lights in house windows; he listened to a dog barking in the distance. What a delightful time he was having.

After carrying this robust little boy for five blocks, I was happy to arrive at the neighborhood church. Sitting down on the front steps, with him on my lap, we watched as a car passed now and again, as a person or two walked by and said hello. I talked with my grandson about the sky, about night, about how much I loved him. He was relaxed, content, and still. Then I sang softly to him for a while. I think we could have spent hours there just enjoying the quiet and softness of the night. Finally, deciding that Grandpa would wonder if we had fallen off the planet, we headed for home.

Needless to say, the little boy was easy to put to bed that night. And he slept peacefully till morning.

Each child is different. How beautiful each one is. And what a joy to get to know each one and what each is all about.

๑

Lord, help me give my grandchildren the encourage-ment and attention they need to maximize their strengths.

PART 8

❧

For My Grandchildren I Will . . .

For My Grandchildren I Will . . .

TELL THE FAMILY HISTORY

🌀

Impress [these commandments, to love God] on your children. Talk about them when you sit at home and when you walk along the road, when you lie down and when you get up.

DEUTERONOMY 6:7

*B*ooks are great and videos are fun. Computers are exciting. Movies can be delightful. But with all those devices and gadgets, who will take time to tell stories to our grandchildren?

Not epic sagas of heroic events but simple, short stories of our past. Stories of daily deeds and common virtues. Tales about our parents and the joys they faced along with the trials and obstacles.

Often we hear an adult who has accomplished something say, "That's one I can tell my grandchildren." We know our children are less likely to hear us out. Parents and children have too many "issues." But grandchildren are another matter. They have great patience to listen as we paint pictures from the past. Grandchildren are eager to know what we consider valuable.

Take a grandchild to the old neighborhood. Give him a sense of context. Let her see the house, the barns, the old church, the water tower, the streetcar tracks, if they are still there.

Tell your grandchildren how you handled race and prejudice in your neighborhood. Anecdotally explain how your parents handled fear and anger. Tell how you celebrated holidays or birthdays, or about some aspect of your courtship and marriage. What attracted you to your spouse—then and still? Tell them what the church and faith meant to your family.

Children will love seeing old photos if you can tell the story of Decker the horse and the time he took off in a run and upset the buggy, dumping great-great-grandma's family. Or another relative who had bushes from his nursery selected for planting at the White House.

When they become teens, they might act as if they don't want to hear. But don't be discouraged. Most young people listen if an adult weaves a truth into a story.

Do you have a story about an honest relative who returned some money because it didn't belong to him or her? Did someone give food to a hungry family? What about the time your family helped clean up a farm after a tornado struck; mother, father, and the children walked the fields picking up glass, nails, wood, and debris so the farmer could plant his crop? Do they know that your family used to sneak around at night and leave groceries in the cars of people who needed food? Have they heard about the Bible studies you used to lead, and maybe still do?

Grandchildren need to know the good deeds and faith that help define the family. Not so we can boast, but so our history will not be a blank. Through our own life and family stories we teach children lessons they won't learn any other way. Maybe even the basic commandments, to love God and neighbor.

You have a story to tell your grandchildren. If they haven't heard it, what's the first chapter they'll soon hear?

ᑐ

Lord, there is so much good to tell; may I be a willing storyteller.

For My Grandchildren I Will . . .

KEEP MYSELF SHARP AND FIT

🌀

Bill's Perspective

May you live to see your children's children.
PSALM 128:6

$\mathcal{E}$very Thursday morning I shave. Like most men, I hate shaving. It takes only a minute, but I still feel a slave to an entirely unnecessary custom. Nonetheless, the day I visit the grandchildren I get up early enough to shave. They deserve better than a skuzzy stubble-faced geezer. If they brush against my skin or look closely at my pink cheeks, I want them to see a smooth surface and a bright complexion.

I keep just a little sharper because I know some wonderful young people. Whenever I get down and blue, I remind myself of the grandchild connection. Children don't need a grumpy pessimist. What a shame if I hand down a dark, ugly view of life. Often I say to myself, "My grandchild deserves a good grandfather." This is the kind of outlook that calls me to ride on top of the waves during all kinds of storms.

We have all met children who hate to hang out with their sour, complaining relatives. We owe our grandchildren much more than a bitter old person living in despair.

They make me want to brush myself off, spread a grin on my face, and ignite a spring in my step. It is for them that I run around the yard, play catch with water balloons, and get

141

down on my hands and knees. I don't want to sit in a rocker and let cobwebs form on my glasses. I want to go to carnivals, climb stairs at the state capitol, and crawl through tunnels at the park.

They make me stay agile. I have to climb trees, take nature hikes, and race across open fields. A guy has to keep moving to do all that.

I take my medicine faithfully. I walk regularly. I eat fruit, oats, and all manner of disgusting health stuff. (OK, I eat sweet snacks too.) I march up all five floors in the parking garage. No, I'm not a fitness nut, but I do take some minimal care. Not for myself alone. Grandchildren keep coming into my life and I need to stay active. They make me want to stay around a little longer.

They make me want to be a better person. For my grandchildren I want to be at my best in a way that parallels my desire to be at my best for my Lord. An old gospel song by Howard Grose starts: "Give of your best to the Master; / Give of the strength of your youth. . . ." As a grandparent I'd rewrite the line to read: "Give of the strength of your age." Any age, even mine.

As Paul said in Philippians 3:15–16: "All of us who are mature should take such a view of things. . . . Let us live up to what we have already attained."

§

Lord, may I give my best to You and to the children You've put in my life.

For My Grandchildren I Will . . .

SAY "THANK YOU FOR COMING"

🌀

Always giving thanks. . . .
EPHESIANS 5:20

"He cries and fights and screams whenever I put him in the car seat," Mommy moaned.

A three-hour trip to Grandpa's house is heavy lifting for the parents. A trip to the other grandparents is even more involved, as it means an across-country airline flight.

Daddy's to-do list is long when it's time to visit grand-parents:

- put things in order at the office
- change oil in the car and go to the car wash
- get the yard in shape
- do the banking
- leave instructions with the neighbor to feed the dog
- pack personal items, clothes, sunglasses, and a book to read
- program the answering machine
- take wheels off the stroller so it fits in the van
- pack the van (thank goodness for a van)
- close up the house

Mommy works for three days getting the laundry caught up and the house in order. Then she must:

- contact someone to teach the Sunday school class
- shampoo and bathe the children

143

- pack clothes, bottles, diapers, books, toys, jackets, toothbrushes, sandals, favorite blankets, snacks
- pack for herself
- exist on four hours sleep the night before the trip and get up early to feed the family
- clean out the refrigerator of what might spoil
- pack the cooler
- take the children to the potty and load them into the van

Whew! Finally they are on the road. Now on to the task of amusing the children who wiggle, get tired of sitting, say, "I'm thirsty," and need to make potty stops. Are we there yet? How many more houses?

When they finally pull into Grandpa's driveway, the children shriek with delight. Bursting through the front door are two grateful grandparents. The fun will now begin.

What a precious gift these generous parents give to Grandma and Grandpa.

With all our hearts, we say, "Thank you, thank you, thank you."

🌀

Lord, may our home always be warm and welcoming so our family wants to come. Remind us always to thank them for making the effort.

For My Grandchildren I Will . . .

BUILD BRIDGES

🌀

"Whoever welcomes one of these little children in my name welcomes me."

MARK 9:37

We may always carry the title of Grandparent, but if we don't make the effort to get to know our children's children, the "grand" won't have the same punch. Not every grandchild will show up one day at a funeral and weep because he or she will miss old Grandpa. Sometimes grandchildren show up and weep because they didn't know him.

Whenever possible, it is good to build the bridges that create trust.

What made me think my grandson would take a trip to Washington, D.C., with me? Why would the young guy agree to get on a plane and fly away from his parents? Frankly, I wasn't 100 percent positive he would. Pretty sure but not positive.

But I knew we had taken the time to build the bridges. We had spent countless hours snapping together model cars and trucks. We had played miniature golf, chased bishops on a chess board, and made up stories together. We had ridden elevators, thrown snowballs, and drawn new continents over breakfast.

We understand each other. We allow for each other's personalities. We grew up together. Kind of.

Trust had been built by time and experience. Like a wooden bridge, we nailed down planks, one at a time. Sometimes we had to replace a board or two with a new one. We weren't too proud to admit we made mistakes.

Building this bridge of trust was easier for us, because we live near each other. Grandparenting is much harder when families are separated by hundreds or thousands of miles. If we stop in every three years and say, "Now, which one is Katie?" the bridge is wobbly and a little scary.

Living far away is sometimes unavoidable. If you have several grown children, it may be impossible to live close to them all. Many, if not most, extended families are separated by miles and have to keep in touch as best they can.

Whenever possible, it is good to build the bridges that create trust.

Don't be surprised if when you walk into a room and say, "Come give Grandpa a hug," that bright-eyed child doesn't rush into your arms. That doesn't say anything bad about the child. It doesn't say anything bad about you. But it might indicate that you need to find a way to build a bridge and close a gap between you. After all, it's hard to run into the arms of a stranger.

First Corinthians 13:7 teaches us that love always perseveres. Children begin in life searching for people they can trust: mothers, fathers, babysitters, practically anyone who will show a caring attitude. They will also trust almost any grandparent figure who is present to them—whether that means stopping by in person or by long distance.

Build a bridge of trust with your grandchild and then walk across it to close the generational divide. Welcome the children into your life. And expect a welcome back.

ᔕ

Lord, help me build bridges of trust that will last a lifetime.

For My Grandchildren I Will . . .

CHANGE EXPECTATIONS

❦

Bill's Perspective

And the child [John] grew and became strong in spirit.
LUKE 1:80

Spring was in the air. It was the time of year to enjoy the outdoors.

Pat and I decided this would be a good time to invite over our eight-year-old grandson. He hadn't visited alone and overnight for several months. He and I could go to the river and explore along the shores and look for nature stuff in the nearby park and maybe go to Fort Kearney and have a picnic or go fishing.

When he was younger, it always delighted us to hear from his mom how he anticipated his visits; he packed all his stuffed animals and was up at 5:00 A.M. on the days when he was coming to our house.

Now Pat and I chose a weekend when our schedule was clear, and we gave him a call.

Not being fond of talking on the phone, his reply was terse; we were not surprised that he said only, "OK, Grandpa."

That evening his dad called. "I don't know why, but he really doesn't want to come. I'm sorry. Please invite him another time."

Our balloon burst.

Like everyone, we are used to no's for various reasons from various people. But our own grandson turning us down knocked our legs out from under us. We were disappointed, confused, and sad.

We can only imagine why he chose not to come. Perhaps he had been too busy going too many places and wanted time at home with his own things. Perhaps things weren't going too well at school, and he just wanted to be with his parents. We'll never know. But the rejection hurt.

This child who had always been eager to do anything with his grandparents was growing up. His world was bigger than just grandparents now.

We enjoy who they are today, not what they were when they were younger or what they may become.

I suppose someday we will have to give up our Thursday visits. When the time comes, we will try to be prepared and move to another phase of our lives. It has already lasted longer than we ever imagined—nine years—and been so much more enjoyable than we could have dreamed. It has been a wonderful journey.

Meanwhile we just enjoy who they are today, not what they were when they were younger or what they may become. They are constantly changing, growing, expanding their horizons, learning, developing, experiencing new things. And we stand back and applaud their lives.

They won't remember all the fun things we did together, nor will we. But our hope is that their souls will be emblazoned with the knowledge that two old folks thought they were precious and wanted to spend time with them. When they were young, excited to be riding an elevator. When they were in elementary school, fascinated with a subway fare-card machine. And when they were—or will be—in junior high,

high school, college, and beyond (should God grant us many years). Only God knows how our relationships will change as we *all* mature.

ᔕ

Lord, may I give my grandchildren the freedom to grow up even if it means that they grow away from me.

For My Grandchildren I Will . . .

PRAY

🌀

I have no greater joy than to hear that my children are walking in the truth.

3 JOHN 4

When our oldest daughter called with the glorious news that a baby was on the way, our hearts rejoiced, and we thanked God and prayed for her safe delivery.

When our first grandson was born, we rejoiced and thanked God again. And prayed for the child.

And now, we've done this five times, once for each new grandchild.

Holding the tiny newborns in our arms, our hearts have nearly burst with praise to a loving heavenly Father.

Driving home after a day with our grandchildren, we sometimes talk about nothing else except what they said or did or what fun the day was, and we thank God for the day.

Many mornings as we individually sit and focus on what really counts in life, we pray for these children, such a precious part of our lives.

Then there was the time when pneumonia struck our one-year-old granddaughter. She clung to her mother, she ached, she cried, she coughed. We were helpless. "Oh, Lord," we prayed, "care for this dear child."

When their grandmother died, we especially prayed for the children and their family.

When flu left them dehydrated and weak, we prayed for help from on high. When one of them broke a wrist, another was rushed to the hospital for stitches... time after time we called out to our God.

When Mommy and Daddy were nearly overwhelmed, we prayed for the family.

And now we watch them as they grow and move out into a world of school and new friends. They are no longer in the safe kindergarten of life, their home.

So much is ahead. No one knows what the future holds. Nothing stays the same. Times change. But we hang onto our heavenly Father who changes not, who is all-knowing, who is always present, and who cares for them with an eternal love. We have hope because we know that God will always be with these dear children.

And we continue to pray... for them, even as we thank God for them.

ᔕ

Lord, we and our grandchildren need You every day. We call out to You, and we rejoice that You always hear our prayers.

NOTE TO THE READER

ABOUT THE AUTHORS

William and Patricia Coleman have three children and five grandchildren who have enriched their lives immeasurably. William is a well-known author of several books, including the best-selling *Before the Ring*.